the roots of reference

the roots of reference

the paul carus lectures

w.v. quine

MOTILAL BANARSIDASS PUBLISHERS
PRIVATE LIMITED • DELHI

First Indian Edition: Delhi, 2009

ISBN: 978-81-208-3365-4

MOTILAL BANARSIDASS
41 U.A. Bungalow Road, Jawahar Nagar, Delhi 110 007
8 Mahalaxmi Chamber, 22 Bhulabhai Desai Road, Mumbai 400 026
203 Royapettah High Road, Mylapore, Chennai 600 004
236, 9th Main III Block, Jayanagar, Bangalore 560 011
Sanas Plaza, 1302 Baji Rao Road, Pune 411 002
8 Camac Street, Kolkata 700 017
Ashok Rajpath, Patna 800 004
Chowk, Varanasi 221 001

PRINTED IN INDIA

By Jainendra Prakash Jain at Shri Jainendra Press,
A-45 Naraina, Phase-I, New Delhi 110 028
and published by Narendra Prakash Jain for
Motilal Banarsidass Publishers Private Limited,
Bungalow Road, Delhi 110 007

To my daughter Norma

contents

preface

Relatively little mystery enshrouds the ways in which we learn to utter observation sentences, and to assent to them or dissent from them when asked. Speaking of objects, however—abstract objects, physical objects, or even sensory objects—is neither so quickly achieved nor so readily accounted for. To speak of objects beyond peradventure the child must master a considerable apparatus of linguistic particles—'same', 'another', 'that', 'it', and the plural '-s', and more—that are inaccessible at the level of observation sentences. In *Word and Object* (p. 93) I wrote that

> the contextual learning of these various particles goes on simultaneously, we may suppose, so that they are gradually adjusted to one another and a coherent pattern of usage is evolved matching that of society. The child scrambles up an intellectual chimney, supporting himself against each side by pressure against the others.

Understandably unsatisfied by so brief and metaphorical an account of the matter, I have pondered it further; and the result is the present essay.

I began it early in 1970, on being invited to give the Paul Carus Lectures at the end of the next year. By the summer of 1971 my ideas had taken the form of a hundred-odd pages of rough draft, and these I expounded in the course of the Summer Institute of Philosophy at Irvine. The lively critical response, especially on the part of Gilbert Harman, Donald Davidson, Oswaldo Chateaubriand, David Kaplan, Richmond Thomason, Edwin A. Martin, Jr., and Stephen Stich, was of great value to me and sparked substantial revisions. Some of my indebtedness is specified at appropriate points in the book. From the revised manuscript I abstracted the three Carus Lectures for oral presentation at a meeting of the American Philosophical Association in New York, December, 1971. Since then I have revised and extended the little book.

I presented portions of an interim draft at Valencia last April in a lecture entitled "Reflexiones sobre el aprendizaje del languaje." This appeared soon after in Teorema. The Hägerström Lectures, which I am to give at Uppsala next month, will be based on the finished book.

I have been helped by comments on various stages of the manuscript from Dagfinn Føllesdal, Richard Herrnstein, Robert Harris, and especially Burton Dreben. The work was supported by the National Science Foundation under Grant GS2615.

W. V. Quine

Boston, December 1972

introduction

By Professor Nelson Goodman
to First Carus Lecture by Professor Quine

The title of Professor Quine's best-known philosophy book is *Word and Object*. From the title of these lectures, I gather he is going to discuss an important relation of words to objects—or better—of words to other objects, some of which are not words—or even better, of objects some of which are words to objects some of which are not words.

I am sure that in every case the exact degree of opacity of reference will be made entirely transparent, even though the roots of reference must be an even dirtier subject than reference itself, which as we all know is dirty enough.

In Professor Quine's many encounters with reference he has always insisted on such sterling principles as: "Don't refer to what isn't"; "Don't suppose that merely by talking you are saying anything about anything"; but on the other hand, "If you do say something about something, don't think you can escape the consequences by saying you were only talking."

I have no idea what the roots of reference are, but I suppose that whatever has powers, as reference does, also has roots. But here I am probably guilty, in the language of *Method of Logic*, of making, in the full sweep of a fell swoop, what amounts to a full swap or even a foul swipe.

Your attention need not be called to Quine's remarkable productivity. In this era of control, it is positively indecent. He gives birth to an important new book more often than the Old Farmer puts out a new Almanac. His articles are by now indenumerable. And it is high time for a meta-anthology drawn from the anthologies of his own works already published.

But my pleasure in yielding the platform to Professor Quine arises not because he is a very distinguished philosopher but because he is a very distinguishing one.

Nelson Goodman

part I
perceiving and learning

§1. *Reception and perception*

Given only the evidence of our senses, how do we arrive at our theory of the world? Bodies are not given in our sensations, but are only inferred from them. Should we follow Berkeley and Hume in repudiating them?

What are given in sensation are smells, noises, feels, flashes, patches of color, and the like: such were the conditions of the problem for Berkeley and Hume. But in the present century the Gestalt psychologists reacted against these conditions. Experiment suggests, and introspection as well, that what are sensed are not primarily those sensory elements, but significantly structured wholes. Confronted with seven spots equally spaced around a center, the subject responds rather to the composite circular form than to any component. Confronted with a solid, he directly senses a body in depth. He goes through none of Berkeley's inferential construction of the depth dimension, for he is unaware of the two-dimensional data of that construction. A painter has to train himself to abstract those two-dimensional patches from the living scene.

Are we to conclude then that the old epistemologists' problem of bridging a gap between sense data and bodies was a pseudoproblem? No, the problem was real but wrongly viewed. The old epistemologists may have thought that their atomistic attitude toward sense data was grounded in introspection, but it was not. It was grounded in their knowledge of the physical world. Berkeley was bent on deriving depth from two-dimensional data for no other reason than the physical fact that the surface of the eye is two-dimensional. But he and the other old epistemologists would have resisted this statement of the matter, because they saw their problem as one of challenging or substantiating our knowledge of the external world. Appeal to physical sense organs in the statement of the problem would have seemed circular. The building blocks had to be irreducibly mental, and present to consciousness. Given these ground rules, the Gestaltists win hands down.

This fear of circularity is a case of needless logical timidity, even granted the project of substantiating our knowledge of the external world. The crucial logical point is that the epistemologist is confronting a challenge to natural science that arises from within natural science. The challenge runs as follows. Science itself teaches that there is no clairvoyance; that the only information that can reach our sensory surfaces from external objects must be limited to two-dimensional optical projections and various impacts of air waves on the eardrums and some gaseous reactions in the nasal passages and a few kindred odds and ends. How, the challenge proceeds, could one hope to find out about that external world from such meager traces? In short, if our science were true, how could we know it? Clearly, in confronting this challenge, the epistemologist may make free use of all scientific theory. His problem is that of finding ways, in keeping with natural science, whereby the human animal can have projected this same science from the sensory information that could reach him according to this science.

Ancient skepticism, in its more primitive way, likewise challenged science from within. The skeptics cited familiar illusions to show the fallibility of the senses; but this concept of illusion itself rested on natural science, since the quality of illusion consisted simply in deviation from external scientific reality.

It was science itself, then as in later times, that demonstrated the limitedness of the evidence for science. And it would have befitted the epistemologist, then as now, to make free use of science in his effort to determine how man could make the most of those limited sources.

Once he recognizes this privilege, the epistemologist can scorn the Gestalt psychologist's strictures against sensory atomism. He can appeal to physical receptors of sensory stimulation and say that for him what is distinctive about sense data is mere proximity to these receptors, without regard to awareness. Better still, he can drop the talk of sense data and talk rather of sensory stimulation. Our liberated epistemologist ends up as an empirical psychologist, scientifically investigating man's acquisition of science.

A far cry, this, from old epistemology. Yet it is no gratuitous change of subject matter, but an enlightened persistence rather in the original epistemological problem. It is enlightened in recognizing that the skeptical challenge springs from science itself, and that in coping with it we are free to use scientific knowledge. The old epistemologist failed to recognize the strength of his position.

The epistemologist thus emerges as a defender or protector. He no longer dreams of a first philosophy, firmer than science, on which science can be based; he is out to defend science from within, against its self-doubts. His project becomes one of major scientific and philosophical interest, moreover, even apart from protective motives—even apart from any thought of a skeptical challenge. For we can fully grant the truth of natural science and still raise the question, within natural science, how it is that man works up his command of that science from the limited impingements that are available to his sensory surfaces. This is a question of empirical psychology, but it may be pursued at one or more removes from the laboratory, one or another level of speculativity. Its philosophical interest is evident. If we were to get to the bottom of it, we ought to be able to see just to what extent science is man's free creation; to what extent, in Eddington's phrase, it is a put-up job. And we ought to be able to see whatever there is to see about the evidence relation, the relation borne to theory by the observations that support it.

We have undercut the Gestalt psychologist's criticism of sensory atomism by dropping the awareness requirement and talking directly of physical input at the sense receptors. This, however, is only half the story. Awareness and Gestalt still claim an important place. Sensory receptors operate at the level of reception, and Gestalt operates at the level of perception. The old antagonism was due to the epistemologist's straining toward reception while still requiring awareness, which belongs to perception.

Reception is flagrantly physical. But perception also, for all its mentalistic overtones, is accessible to behavioral criteria. It shows itself in the conditioning of responses. Thus suppose we provide an animal with a screen to look at and a lever to press. He finds that the pressed lever brings a pellet of food when the screen shows a circular stripe, and that it brings a shock when the screen shows merely four spots spaced in a semicircular arc. Now we present him with those same four spots, arranged as before, but supplemented with three more to suggest the complementary semicircle. If the animal presses the lever, he may be said to have perceived the circular Gestalt rather than the component spots.

When conceived thus in behavioral terms, the notion of perception belongs to the psychology of learning: to the theory of conditioning, or of habit formation. Habits, inculcated by conditioning, are dispositions. The subject, having learned his lesson, is thereafter disposed to make the response in question whenever activated by the stimulus in question. We shall do well, then, before venturing further, to come to terms with the notion of a disposition.

§2. *Cause*

There is an evident affinity between the idioms of cause and disposition. Solubility in water, for instance, is the disposition to dissolve in water; and being in water causes the soluble body to dissolve. In their combination of utility and disreputability, moreover, the two idioms are much alike. The trouble with causation is, as Hume pointed out, that there is no evident way of distinguishing it from mere invariable sucession. And why is *this* troublesome? Because then, if we take any two classes of events such that each event in the one class is followed by an event in the other, we have to say that the events in the one class cause those in the other. Thereupon any arbitrary event *a* can be said to have caused any succeeding event *b*; for, we can just take the two classes as the unit classes of *a* and *b*. We are caught in the fallacy of *post hoc ergo propter hoc*.

There is the same quandary over dispositions. If there is no distinguishing between a thing's disposition to act in a certain way in certain circumstances and the mere fact of its so acting in those circumstances, then whatever the thing may do can be laid to a disposition, by defining the circumstances narrowly enough.

Stephen Stich has made this point strikingly with reference to innate dispositions. Why not attribute a man's every act to an innate disposition? True, if the circumstances in which he now acts in a certain way are circumstances in which he once failed so to act, we seem to have grounds for denying an innate disposition; but the trouble is that any circumstances whatever can be said to be of an unprecedented kind by defining the kind narrowly.

Of these two wayward idioms, the causal and the dispositional, the causal is the simpler and the more fundamental. It may have had its prehistoric beginnings in man's sense of effort, as in pushing. The imparting of energy still seems to be the central idea. The transfer of momentum from one billiard ball to another is persistently cited as a paradigm case of causality. Thus we might seek a simpleminded or root notion of causality in terms of the flow of energy. Cause and effect are events such that all the energy in the effect flowed from the cause. This thermodynamical image requires us to picture energy, like matter, as traceable from point to point through time. Thus let us picture an event simply as any fragment of space-time, or the material and energetic content thereof. Given an event *e*, then, imagine all its energy traced backward through time. Any earlier event that intercepts all of these energetic world lines qualifies as a cause of *e*.

According to this account each event *e* has countless causes, distributed over past time. The remoter the cause, usually, the more diffuse it will be in space, since it must intercept every energetic world line that is destined to get into *e*.

Let us now sort out the good and the bad features of this notion of cause. A possible objection is that it is too special, applying only to physics. My answer is materialistic. Causality is a relation of events, and all events, mental and social ones included, are a matter ultimately of the action of physical forces upon particles. My concern here is different from Hume's; his was with the epistemological basis for a causal relation, while mine is with the ontological nature of the causal relation as an object of scientific theory. All will agree, materialists and others, that causal efficacy within the material world, at any rate, is compounded of microphysical forces, despite our incapacity to single out all those components in every particular case.

Another possible objection is that my appeal to energy and world lines is too sophisticated to be appropriate in explicating so primordial a notion of common sense as the notion of cause. My answer is that we may reasonably allow concepts, however primordial, to evolve and sharpen with the progress of science. After all, even the scope or subject matter of a science may not be definable until the science has made great strides; so it was with chemistry. Let the explication of causality not be hampered by restraints on the use of sophisticated scientific notions.

A third and opposite objection, and one that I can share, is that my appeal to energetic world lines is not sophisticated enough. On what basis can an earlier and a later bit of work be associated as two manifestations of one and the same continuing bit of energy? The very distinction between matter and energy wavers in modern physics, and even the notion of the identity of an elementary particle from moment to moment has fallen on evil days, what with quantum jumps. Now I take this consideration to suggest simply that a notion of cause is out of place in modern physics. Nor can this come as a surprise. Clearly the term plays no technical role at austere levels of the subject. And anyway, modern physicists are notorious for scouting primordial concepts. They have taken away our absolute time dimension, our absolute simultaneity. They have taken away even our relative velocity, or further relativized it. They have put limits on divisibility, on velocity, on antiquity, and even on theoretical exactness of position and velocity. Taking away our causality is the least of it.

For moderate velocities and respectable magnitudes, however, the Newtonian mechanics retains its utility despite relativity and quantum mechanics. For terrestrial concerns even the geocentric frame of reference retains its utility despite Copernicus. Similarly a notion of cause based on the not very sophisticated notion of the flow of energy, or thermodynamics, could retain utility.

Precisely this utility, however, is called into question by a fourth objection. The proposed explication covers only total cause. It does assign multiple causes, as we saw, but each of them is total in this sense: each of them intercepts all the energetic lines that lead into the effect. These total causes differ from one another only in date or duration or in the capricious inclusion of superfluities. Yet *contributory* cause, rather than total cause, is what we usually care about in practice. The catalyst introduces little energy into the chemical reaction that it sets off. The killer introduces little energy of his own when he triggers the fatal explosion in his gun. The speaker imparts little energy to the hearer's eardrum, yet his words may spur the hearer to a frenzy of energetic output.

We can accommodate contributory causes by defining them as intercepting merely some of the energetic lines that lead into the effect. But one's interest in contributory causes is conspicuously independent of the proportion of energy contributed. Overwhelming sources such as solar radiation will commonly be passed over because taken for granted. When in practice we ask the cause of something, or cite the cause, we are concerned only with some contributory cause that is of especial interest to the context. All the rest of a total cause may be uninteresting because already known; this one contributory part is all that was needed to complete our understanding of the case. Or the rest of the total cause may be uninteresting because it would be immaterial to some practical end, such as allocation of responsibility.

In practice, indeed, the words 'cause' and 'because' often connote no contribution of energy at all. They are stretched to apply to logical premisses, to purposes, to dispositions. Something's merely being paper, or salt, is seen as a contributory cause of its taking fire, or dissolving in water. But all this strikes me as extended usage, contribution of energy being the kernel idea. Of the extended usage, a large part is best viewed under the head rather of dispositions.

§3. *Disposition*

The proposed thermodynamical conception of cause does some justice to the notion of cause on its theoretical or philosophical side, and it makes sense to the extent that a notion of energy flow makes sense. This is better than we can evidently hope to achieve in a theoretical account of the notion of disposition. For, even supposing the notion of cause to be in acceptable theoretical shape, how would we define disposition in terms of it? The disposition is a property, in the object, by virtue of which the circumstances *c* cause the object to do *a*. The 'by virtue' here is what defies explication. An extensional conditional, a universally quantified material conditional, does not bridge the gap. Thus consider a gold piece that is destined never to be in water. The familiar point is that though we may vacuously and truly say in an extensional sense that the gold piece dissolves whenever in water, we are not therefore to count it soluble. Now the further point to note is that even an appeal to cause does not mend matters. For we can equally well say of the gold piece, vacuously and truly, that whenever it is in water its being in water *causes* it to dissolve. The perennial falsity of the antecedent of this universally quantified material conditional has its trivializing effect regardless of whether we talk of cause in the consequent. Cause is not the missing link.

Where the strong connection is wanted is between the disposition (solubility in water) and its realization (dissolving when in water). The body dissolves when in water by virtue of having the disposition. The "virtual" connection is itself analogous to a causal one; 'by virtue of ' is almost 'because of '. But whereas we were afforded some hint of an explication of cause in the flow of energy from cause to effect, we can in general look to no such flow from the disposition to its realization.

At an uncritical level the usual paraphrase of the disposition idiom is an intensional conditional. To say that a body is soluble in water is to say that it *would* dissolve if it *were* in water. This strengthened conditional does its work at a curious remove. Where the problematic link 'by virtue of' was needed was for linking 'solubility in water' with 'dissolves when in water'. But the intensional conditional, the 'would if were', visibly links the dissolving rather with the being in water. This is not where a strengthened link was needed; cause, we noted, was not the missing link. Yet there is no denying that in its bumbling way this intensional conditional somehow conveys the force of the dispositional idiom.

There are those who uncritically accept the dispositional idiom as a clear matter of ordinary language. Say what a thing is disposed to do in what circumstances, and the disposition holds no further mystery for them. Solubility in water is the disposition to dissolve when in water, and there is no plainer English than that. Such is Ryle's position in *The Concept of Mind*, where he undertakes to clarify other more obscure and troublesome notions in dispositional terms and is content to leave them thus. Again there are those who acquiesce in the general definition of the dispositional idiom in terms of the intensional conditional. This group is not to be distinguished from the other, since the dispositional idiom and the corresponding conditional are interchangeable in ordinary language as a matter of course.

One who finds discomfort in intensional conditionals is at a loss for a satisfactory definition of the dispositional idiom. It was on this account that Carnap, in his extensionalist period,[1] resorted to a theory of so-called "reduction forms," as a means of introducing terms into a theory by partial explications short of definition. These explications were partial in that they were insufficient to render the terms eliminable, as true definitions would do. They were "meaning postulates," in Carnap's later terminology. His reduction form or meaning postulate for

1. "Testability and meaning."

solubility in water stipulated that if a body is in water, then it is soluble in water if and only if it is dissolving. The reduction form for the disposition to do *a* in circumstances *c* stipulated that if something is in circumstances *c* then it has the disposition if and only if it is doing *a*.

Thus Carnap, like Ryle, acquiesced in an undefined notion of disposition, but unlike Ryle he acquiesced grudgingly. The notion of disposition was short on meaning, in Carnap's eyes, to the degree that the "reduction form" or "meaning postulate" stopped short of definition.

I am with Carnap in not settling for definition of dispositions by the intensional conditional. Unlike Carnap, however, I am not concerned to establish the disposition idiom as a technical idiom of scientific theory at all, either by hook or by crook: either by definition or by "meaning postulate."

Each disposition, in my view, is a physical state or mechanism. A name for a specific disposition, e.g. solubility in water, deserves its place in the vocabulary of scientific theory as a name of a particular state or mechanism. In some cases, as in the case nowadays of solubility in water, we understand the physical details and are able to set them forth explicitly in terms of the arrangement and interaction of small bodies. Such a formulation, once achieved, can thenceforward even take the place of the old disposition term, or stand as its new definition.

Where the general dispositional idiom has its use is as follows. By means of it we can refer to a hypothetical state or mechanism that we do not yet understand, or to any of various such states or mechanisms, while merely specifying one of its characteristic effects, such as dissolution upon immersion in water. There are dispositions, such as intelligence, whose physical workings we can scarcely conjecture; the dispositional characterization is all we have to go on. Intelligence is the disposition to learn quickly, if I may oversimplify. By intelligence I still mean some attribute of the body, despite our ignorance concerning it; some durable physical state, perhaps a highly disjunctive one. A term for this attribute is entitled to a place in our theoretical vocabulary, even if all we know about the attribute is that an animal that has it is quickly conditioned. After all, we do not restrict our theoretical vocabulary to things we understand completely. Ignorance is everywhere, and is a matter of degree.

I remarked that the flow of energy characteristic of cause is not characteristic of disposition. Still it is not excluded. The dispositions are hypothetical physical states or mechanisms, and the mechanisms will pass energy.

Terms for specific dispositions have a legitimate place, then, in the theoretical vocabulary. As theory progresses, some of these terms can be paraphrased, like 'water soluble', into terms of the mechanics of small bodies. Others, like 'intelligent', may stay on as uneliminable components of a few theoretical statements. The *general* dispositional idiom, however, may best be viewed as external to these growing theories in which the particular cases of the dispositional idiom turn up. By 'the general dispositional idiom' I mean the general technique of applying the suffix '-ile' or '-ble' to verb stems and of using the word 'disposition' and, for that matter, the corresponding intensional conditional. This general idiom is programmatic; it plays a regulative rather than a constitutive role. It forms families of terms on the basis not of structural or causal affinities among the physical states or mechanisms that the terms refer to, but on the basis only of a sameness of style on our own part in earmarking those states or mechanisms. The suffix '-ile' or '-ble' in 'soluble', 'portable', 'visible', 'ductile', 'fragile', 'combustible', and 'comestible' connote a sameness in the style of the cues or tests that we are offering for recognizing or identifying these seven physical attributes. "Put the thing into water and see if it dissolves," "heft it and see if you can carry it," "face it and see if you can see it," and so on. The seven physical attributes that are more or less recognized through these cues can be conveyed in further detail in terms of size, shape, density, and minute physicochemical structure, and there is no significant physical principle that sets the seven apart from others. The dispositional idiom is indifferent to the physical subject matter and serves only to signal how we are getting at it.

So, if I were trying to devise an ideal language for a finished theory of reality, or of any part of it, I would make no place in it for the general dispositional idiom. In developing a theory, on the other hand, the idiom is indispensable. Just as in writing an essay one commonly sketches various ulterior paragraphs before completing the front ones, so in developing a theory one sketches in a few key traits of what is meant ultimately to emerge as a satisfactorily explanatory mechanism. Such is the role of the general dispositional idiom. And since scientific theory is always developing, the idiom is here to stay.

§4. *Some questions and answers on dispositions*

An infirmity of the dispositional idiom, or the intensional conditional, is its dependence on a vague proviso of *caeteris paribus*. The usual disposition is not surefire. Will anything that is soluble in water unfailingly dissolve when in water, or must we make allowance for low temperatures and high ionization and other possible interferences as yet unforeseen? One expedient that has been suggested for accommodating this difficulty is a retreat to probability:[1] anything that is soluble in water will probably dissolve when in water. Now one is bound to agree to the truth of this probability statement, but it raises questions when proposed as a means of explication. What sort of probability is intended? If it is subjective probability in some sense, then this explication of solubility seems wide of the mark; solubility should be a physical property of the soluble body, even when only dimly understood. Or if objective probability is intended, hence relative frequency, then what is the reference class? Evidently the class of all soluble bodies; but that was what we wanted explained. Perhaps the fair answer is that this probability statement is meant only as a partial explication of a strictly undefined disposition term, on a par with Carnap's reduction form.

Carnap's own response to the *caeteris paribus* problem was different: not a resort to probability, but a recognition that his reduction form could be seen as at best an instructive idealization, because of its unqualified demand that anything soluble in water dissolve when in water. If the progress of science were to

1. E.g. see the quotation from Chomsky a page or two hence.

reveal the need of exceptions for low temperatures or other circumstances, the reduction form might be fitted out with added complexities to accommodate them. Now in this matter Carnap's view resembles the one I am urging: the view of a disposition as a partially discerned physical property that will be more fully identified, we hope, as science progresses. But a conspicuous difference in our views is that for him all such patching and adjusting of reduction forms was something like redefinition, giving rise to newly analytic sentences, sentences true by the meanings of the words. I, on the other hand, am invoking no distinction between analytic sentences and others.

A quandary of Stich's over innate dispositions was noted early in §2. What can be said of innate dispositions now? When I posit an innate disposition I am assuming some specific though unspecified arrangement of cells or perhaps some combination of such arrangements. It could be a nerve tract or a gland. It could consist of several structures, variously situated in the organism. It could be one structure in one individual and some different structure to the same specified effect in another individual. Its innateness consists in its being complete at birth.

Innate reflexes, Holt has well argued, are no different in kind from postnatally conditioned reflexes. To acquire a reflex is to acquire a neural path of lowered resistance; according to my philosophy of dispositions, indeed, that path *is* the reflex. Some such paths are established by reinforcement of random movements of the infant, and others, according to Holt, by reinforcement of random movements of the foetus. The innate dispositions, then, are a mixed bag: innate reflexes are learned *in utero*, while innate dispositions of deeper sorts are handed down from generation to generation through genetic coding in the chromosome. They are a mixed lot of structures, specified primarily by what they make the animal do in what circumstances, and grouped together by the accident of being complete at birth.

The attribution of a behavioral disposition, learned or unlearned, is a physiological hypothesis, however fragmentary. It is the assumption of some physiological arrangement such that, if we were ever to succeed in identifying and analyzing it, we should arrive at a satisfactory understanding of the mechanism of the animal behavior in question.

I have described the primary role, as I see it, of the dispositional idiom. The idiom is handy also, though not indispensable, in historical contexts. Thus take again the example of solubility in water. Some scientist's discoveries have enabled us to specify this physical attribute in microphysical terms, thus bypassing the verb stem and dispositional suffix. But how is the historian to give this scientist his due, once solubility itself is redefined as nothing other than this microphysical equivalent? He gives him his due, of course, by cleaving to the naively dispositional sense of the disposition term. This, however, is a minor practical point, since the historian would find no difficulty in describing the scientist's contribution without resorting to the dispositional idiom. He has only to say that the scientist showed that any substance endowed with the microphysical structure in question will dissolve when in water, and any substance not so endowed will fail to dissolve when in water.

I once expressed my view of dispositions by saying that a disposition term is a promissory note for an eventual description in mechanical terms. Goodman noted (p. 45n) that these mechanistic terms will in the last analysis probably be implicitly dispositional in turn, thus affording no escape from the circle. This objection neatly brings out a difference between my attitude toward the problem and the attitude of both Carnap and Goodman. They were seeing the problem as that of defining or somehow explicating the dispositional idiom in a more strictly empirical idiom. The circularity apprehended by Goodman would matter there. I, on the other hand, am content to rest with a theoretical vocabulary some of whose primitive physical predicates were first learned with help of the dispositional idiom. Nor am I bent on finding a respectable place for the general dispositional idiom in a regimented theoretical language. I describe the heuristic role of that idiom in the working up of a scientific theory, and then I use it.

There are two curious criticisms that I would briefly take up before closing this general discussion of dispositions, lest the misconceptions that underlie them be shared by any present readers. Ziff observes, rightly enough, that every sentence that a man is capable of using or understanding must correspond to a distinct disposition on his part and therefore, on my view, to some distinct mechanism or enduring condition in his body. Ziff finds it implausible that there should be so many distinct mechanisms or concurrent physical conditions in the body. Now the reason it is not implausible is that we are not to imagine countless discrete mechanisms side by side, nor physical states of discrete parts of the body, one for every sentence. The several mechanisms certainly share their parts, much as the sentences themselves share their vocabulary and share their grammatical constructions. One wonders, indeed, what alternative Ziff has in mind. If two men now were physically exactly alike down to the smallest particle, might there be a sentence that the one man is now capable of understanding and the other man not? Maybe the trouble was a confusion between distinctness of mechanisms and discreteness of mechanisms.

The other point was Chomsky's, in reference to my "definition of 'language' as a 'complex of dispositions to verbal behavior.' "

> Presumably, a complex of dispositions is a structure that can be represented as a set of probabilities for utterances in certain definable "circumstances" or "situations." But it must be recognized that the notion "probability of a sentence" is an entirely useless one. . . . On empirical grounds, the probability of my producing some given sentence of English . . . is indistinguishable from the probability of my producing a given sentence of Japanese. (P. 57.)

Let us not forget that dispositions have their conditions. The probability that a given lump of salt will dissolve at time *t* is as may be, but the probability that it will dissolve if immersed in water is high. Chomsky's worry may have been a more specific difficulty: that of setting conditions for the triggering of verbal dispositions. This is an important problem, and happily it has an easy solution—a solution, indeed, that was prominent in the book that Chomsky was commenting on. It is the procedure of query and assent, which I shall take up in §12.

§5. *Similarity*

Having reflected on the general notion of disposition, let us return now to the notion of perception; for that was what brought dispositions up. The animal had been trained to press the lever when confronted with the circular stripe and to refrain from pressing it when confronted with the four spots. Then, when he was confronted with the seven spots, his pressing of the lever was the criterion of his perceiving the circular Gestalt.

But we gain flexibility if, instead of speaking thus flatly of what is or is not perceived, we allow for differences of degree. This can be done by speaking of perceptual similarity; thus the configuration of seven spots proves to be perceptually more similar to the circular stripe, for this animal, than to the configuration of four spots. Better still, we may take perceptual similarity as relating moments or brief episodes of the subject's life.

This shift from perceptions to perceptual similarity brings not only flexibility but also a certain gain in ontological clarity, by dismissing the percepts or perceptions. Ontologically the episodes that are related by perceptual similarity may be understood simply as brief stages or temporal segments of the perceiving subject's body. They are times in his life. Thus they are global episodes, including all irrelevancies. But the perceptual similarity that relates them is no overall point-by-point similarity. It can be as partial as you please, focussing on where the action is.

Readers familiar with Carnap's *Aufbau* will be reminded here of his *Elementarerlebnisse* and *Aehnlichkeitserinnerung*. The parallel is no accident.

A theory of perceptual similarity, then, is the place for Gestalt principles. Perceptual similarity contrasts with *receptual* similarity; this is mere physical similarity of impact on the sensory surfaces, regardless of behavior. Both of these similarity relations may be viewed to begin with as triadic: episode *a* is more similar to *b* than to *c*. Episodes are receptually similar to the degree that the total set of sensory receptors that are triggered on the one occasion approximates the set triggered on the other occasion. Perceptual similarity, on the other hand, is a bundle of second-order dispositions to behavior. Rather than try to define the notion at this stage, let us take it provisionally as a theoretical notion about which some substantial things can be said. Reflecting on the example of the circular stripe and the spots, we see how perceptual similarity is manifested in behavior.

To explain how, we are apt to say that an episode *a* is proved to be perceptually more similar to *b* than to *c* when the subject has been conditioned to respond in some fashion to *b* and not to so respond to *c*, and then is found to respond in that fashion to *a*. But let us remember that *a, b,* and *c* are individual dated concrete occasions in the subject's life, whereas conditioning is directed rather to repeatable types of occasions.

This discrepancy can be corrected by enlisting the aid of receptual similarity, so as to appeal not just to unique episodes *a, b,* and *c*, but more generally to episodes that are receptually similar to these. Now receptual similarity is, we know, a matter of degree. Full receptual identity would never be realized, or, if realized, recognized; for it would be a triggering of all and only the same sensory receptors on the subject's surface on both occasions, no surface barred. However, the mathematical idea of a neighborhood can be put to use here.

The term 'neighborhood' is one that makes sense only in special contexts, and the key word of those contexts is 'all'. When we attribute some property to *all* points in the *neighborhood* of a point *p*, we mean, in the vernacular, that every point "sufficiently near to *p*" has the property; or, to be quite explicit, we mean that there is a point *q* that is distinct from *p* and is such that every point that is nearer to *p*, than *q* is, has the property. Applying this idea to receptual similarity, let us attribute a property to *all episodes in the receptual neighborhood* of an episode *a* when what we mean is that there is an episode *d* that is not receptually identical with *a* and is such that every episode that is receptually more similar to *a*, than *d* is, has the property in question.

Now we can correct our formulation of the behavioral condition for perceptual similarity, to read thus: *a* is shown to be perceptually more similar to *b* than to *c* when the subject has been conditioned to respond in some fashion to all episodes in the receptual neighborhood of *b*, and to withhold that response from all those in the receptual neighborhood of *c*, and is then found to so respond to those in the neighborhood of *a*.

Perceptual similarity is a question of the subject's disposition to submit to conditioning in one way and another; hence of his disposition to acquire or change his habits of response. These habits are themselves dispositions to behavior, and thus it is that perceptual similarity is a bundle of second-order dispositions to behavior.

Perceptual similarity is no doubt a very disconnected relation. That is, there would be many episodes for which it would make no evident or useful sense to say that this one was perceptually more or less similar to that one than to the other. For that matter, we cannot consider ourselves to have *defined* perceptual similarity even for the best of cases. For such cases I have propounded a behavioral condition that is a sufficient condition but not a necessary one. We can console ourselves for this want of definition by recalling our general reflections on dispositions. This behavioral condition for perceptual similarity serves merely to earmark a hypothetical mechanism in terms of one of its key traits.

My characterization of perceptual similarity as triadic—*a* is more similar to *b* than to *c*—can be depended upon to have triggered in the reader's mind the more general tetradic idea: *a* is more similar to *b* than *c* is to *d*. Pursuing this idea, the reader will have noticed that our way of experimentally testing for perceptual similarity comparisons of the triadic kind admits of no obvious extension to the tetradic. Nor do I see a need for this tetradic relation, in a theory of learning.

There is reason, however, for a polyadic extension of another form: *a* is more similar to $b_1, \ldots, b_m$ than to $c_1, \ldots, c_n$. Thus, to anticipate an example that will receive closer attention in §8, let us imagine a certain response reinforced in the presence of a red ball and penalized in the presence of a yellow rose. A red rose, then, will perhaps not elicit the response, given its favorable color but unfavorable shape. But if the response was reinforced also in the presence of a red shawl, the red rose will elicit it. So we do not want to say that the episode of the red rose was perceptually more similar to that of the red ball than to that of the yellow rose, but we do want to say that it was perceptually more similar jointly to the episodes of the red ball and the red shawl than to that of the yellow rose.

One is inclined to distinguish *respects* of perceptual similarity; thus shape versus color. This complication is convenient in practice, but I think it is dispensable in theory, by spreading the similarity polyadically as in the above example.

Let us now turn away from the logical technicalities and contemplate the importance of the relation of perceptual similarity. If an individual learns at all, differences in degree of similarity must be implicit in his learning pattern. Otherwise any response, if reinforced, would be conditioned equally and indiscriminately to any and every future episode, all these being equally similar. Some implicit standard, however provisional, for ordering our episodes as more or less similar must therefore antedate all learning, and be innate.

Perceptual similarity is always confined within an individual; the episodes that it relates are episodes in his life, and they are more and less similar for him. One cannot easily give meaning, indeed, to a general objective similarity relation among things in the world. Might we say that a thing is more similar to one than another if it shares more properties with the one than with the other? But what counts as a property? Classes, certainly, show no favorites; a thing shares no more class-membership with any one thing than with any other.

Yet the innate sense of perceptual similarity has, for all its subjectivity, a degree of objective validity. After all, man's inductive expectations are reached by extrapolating along lines of perceptual similarity: experiences that begin similarly are expected to turn out in similar ways. Our innate standards of perceptual similarity show a gratifying tendency to run with the grain of nature. This concurrence is accountable, surely, to natural selection. Since good prediction has survival value, natural selection will have fostered perceptual similarity standards in us and in other animals that tend accordingly. Natural selection will have favored green and blue, as avenues of inductive generalization, and never grue.[1]

These thoughts are not meant to *justify* induction. For that

1. See Goodman, pp. 74-100.

purpose the appeal to a law of natural selection would be unwarranted, since that law rests in turn on induction. In the matter of justifying induction we are back with Hume, where we doubtless belong. Asking for a justification of induction is like asking for a first philosophy in support of science. What natural selection contributes, rather, in the foregoing argument, is a reason why induction works, granted that it does. We have here, indeed, an illustrative part of an answer to what we recognized earlier as the central question of enlightened epistemology: how, if our theory of the external world is true, could we ever hit upon it?

§6. *Interference from within*

We saw that some implicit standards of perceptual similarity must be innate. The standards change markedly, however, with experience.

> Pavlov . . . mentions an experiment that can easily be interpreted as the acquisition of a similarity sensation between three stimuli. A dog was subjected to three types of pairing situations in which the sound of a buzzer, the sound of a metronome, and a tactile stimulus were paired with food. . . . Later, one of these stimuli was inhibited and it was observed that the inhibition generalized to the other two stimuli.[1]

Because of this instability of one's standards of perceptual similarity, a problem arises over what to count as perceptual similarity at all. To appreciate this problem, remember that a subject's standards of perceptual similarity are to be known only from his behavior. Some response on his part was reinforced on occasion *b* and penalized on occasion *c* and then elicited on occasion *a*, and this is supposed to show that *a* was perceptually more similar to *b* for him than to *c*. Now the trouble with this criterion is that it does not screen out the possible effects of the internal states, however transitory, that the subject was enjoying when these impingements overtook him. What of his current purposes,

1. Stemmer, p. 211. His reference is to Pavlov, pp. 55f.

his passing memories, his interrupted train of thought? I speak mentalistically, but I refer to factors of his physical state, whatever their physical mechanism. These factors could encourage or inhibit the response in question, on occasion *a* or *b* or *c*, overriding the force of current impingements. How to make proper allowance for these internal interferences is a delicate problem, for we do not want to screen out the subject's actual contribution to perception.

Episodes in the subject's life ought, one feels, to admit of three sorts of similarity. There is receptual similarity, having to do only with sensory input. There is behavioral similarity, at the other extreme, which relates episodes according to the output of overt behavior at those times, regardless of causal factors. A theoretical definition of behavioral similarity is readily imagined. It might be sought in terms of the total set of fibres of striped muscle that are contracted or released on one occasion and on another, or a more functional approach might be devised. Perceptual similarity, finally, should be somehow intermediate between receptual and behavioral similarity. It should be reflected in the behavioral output of the episode rather than just current input, but it should be reflected in only so much of the behavioral output as is somehow distinctive to the current input.

However fully the subject's present inner life is determined by the totality of past impingements, it is not determined by present ones. This is why similar behavior is not in general to be expected in receptually similar episodes. But perceptual similarity is not to be expected of receptually similar episodes either, because of changes in standards of perceptual similarity, changes in second-order dispositions. So, if a response that was reinforced on occasion *b* and penalized on occasion *c* is elicited on occasion *a*, how are we to judge whether *a* is indeed more similar to *b* than to *c* by the subject's current perceptual standards, or whether some perceptually irrelevant internal state has intruded? Our trouble is that we are groping for a notion of perception just here, with no other to check against.

The notion of perceptual similarity seemed straightforward enough when we were considering the animal experiment. We reward a response in one situation and penalize it in another and then check for it in a third. This idea was the basis for the explication of perceptual similarity that we undertook in §5. As usual where dispositions are concerned, the explication was partial: a purportedly sufficient condition for perceptual similarity in behavioral terms. Now we are finding, as is usual where dispositions are concerned, that our behavioral condition is not hard and fast even as a sufficient condition. It bogs down in the *caeteris paribus* effect (§4). This happens, we know, to the best of dispositions: interferences intrude. But then it is our job to look for ways of screening out such interferences as best we can.

In practice this is scarcely a problem. We might explore a human subject's similarity standards simply by asking him which of various pairs of stimuli are more alike, thus trusting his inarticulate sense of what interferences to screen out. Or, using more cunning, we might condition some reflexes; and in this event we would circumvent any likely interferences by dint of an inarticulate sense of our own. Theory, however, must be articulate. What are we sorting out?

At this point some heuristic value can be got from evolutionary considerations. There must be, we saw, an innate standard of perceptual similarity. It underlies our primitive inductions, and is accountable to natural selection by virtue of its survival value. So we may be confident that what we are looking for under the head of perceptual similarity must persist rather stably, and manifest itself in the subject's behavior a good part of the time, despite sporadic interferences from his ongoing internal states. If it were not thus dominant and persistent, it would not have been so important for survival; it would not have helped our ancestors so much in recognizing the wholesome and the toxic, the predator and the prey. Moreover, such being the nature of this hypothetical physiological state or mechanism, we may expect it to change only slowly under the influence of experience.

These reflections suggest how one might in principle distinguish between the perceptually relevant episodes, as we might call them, and the episodes in which the behavior is due largely to internal interference. If an episode is perceptually relevant, then *most* episodes that are not very remote in time from that one, and are receptually similar to it, should be behaviorally similar to it. These perceptually relevant episodes are the ones to count in gauging a subject's standards of perceptual similarity. It is a matter of detecting regular trends beneath the perturbations. One is reminded of Fourier analysis of wave patterns, though matters are vaguer here.

The same considerations of innateness and natural selection suggest also another and better index of what behavior to reckon to perceptual similarities. Namely, we can count on considerable social uniformity in perceptual similarity standards. We may expect our innate similarity standards to be much alike, since they are hereditary in the race; and even as these standards gradually change with experience we may expect them to stay significantly alike, what with our shared environment, shared culture, shared language, and mutual influence. So, if we find that one subject's episodes *a* and *b* tend to be perceptually more or less similar according as another subject's episodes *a*′ and *b*′ are perceptually more or less similar, wherever *a* is receptually very similar to *a*′ and *b* to *b*′, we may be encouraged to believe that our plotting of perceptual similarities for these two subjects is proceeding nicely.

Perception being such a private business, I find it ironical that the best evidence of what to count as perceptual should be social conformity. I shall not pause over the lesson, but there is surely one there.

A certain lacuna must be acknowledged, however, in this matter of *a*, *b*, *a*′, and *b*′. Receptual similarity was defined in §5 in terms of how close the class of all the receptors that were activated in one episode came to matching the class of those activated in another episode. At that point we were thinking of the episodes and receptors as all belonging to one subject. But now we have appealed to receptual similarity between episodes *a* and *a*′ of two subjects. The subjects share no receptors, so it is no longer a question of matching the two classes of receptors on the score of their sharing most of their members. It becomes a question rather of how nearly homologous, anatomically, most of the members of one class are with those of the other. Vagueness mounts, since the receptors of different subjects are far from homologous.[2] Nor is anything to be gained by trying rather to match the distribution of the external forces impinging on the two subjects; for we would have to require that the subjects be oriented alike to the impingement pattern, and this revives the homology question. In practice, of course, psychologists find no difficulty in such intersubjective equating of stimulus situations; they simply see that there are no physical differences that are apt to matter. We shall do well to take the same line, having just noted in passing that there is more to the equating of stimulations than meets the eye, or indeed perhaps rather less than seems to do so.

§7. *Traces and salience*

Episodes leave traces. Memory is a case in point. I shall not here discuss memory as such, for that concept covers too broad and diffuse a range of phenomena to be helpful in an analysis of the learning process. We of course cannot avoid positing various hypothetical mechanisms, partially specifying them by their required effects and leaving their physical mode of operation undetermined. But it behooves us to keep these functional specifications as simple and specific as we can, in hopes of hastening the day when their physical mode of operation may be understood. Such posits may in part fall within the broad range of what one calls memory, but they will be more limited.

A subject's perceptual similarities are reflected in his behavior: in the reinforcement and extinction of his responses: in a word, in his learning. Perceptual similarity relates his present episode to a past episode. If perceptual similarity is to have its required effect on his present behavior, then, or indeed any effect on anything, the subject must harbor some physiological condition that was brought about by that past episode. Otherwise that episode

2. Nerve nets differ markedly in structure from one member of a species to another even at the level of insects. "I should never have expected that the branching of the main nerves close to the great central ganglion of an insect would have been variable in the same species; . . . yet quite recently Mr. Lubbock has shown a degree of variability in these main nerves in Coccus, which may almost be compared to the irregular branching of the stem of a tree." (Darwin, pp. 45f.)

would be lost to present perceptual comparison. Such *traces*, whatever their physiological nature, are essential to all learning. The trace of an episode must preserve, in some form, enough information to show perceptual similarity between that episode and later ones. (Recall again Carnap's *Aehnlichkeitserinnerung*.)

Each episode, it will be recalled, is a brief time in the life of the subject in his bodily entirety. All impingement is included, sparing no bodily surface. The trace of course preserves no such full information, nor would much of it be useful for perceptual similarity. For it is only receptual similarity that accepts all the activated receptors on an equal footing, unrestricted to what the subject notices. Perceptual similarity hinges more on noticing, and so it is with traces.

Noticing is a matter of degree, and perceptual similarity is sensitive to this variation. Thus suppose a cat is visible at times *a*, *b*, and *c*; suppose that the broad visual setting of the cat is much the same at times *a* and *c* but quite different at *b*; but suppose the cat is salient at times *a* and *b*, because of motion or spotlighting or focal position, and not at *c*. Then the subject may find *a* perceptually more similar to *b* than to *c*, despite the sameness of landscape at *a* and *c*. Perhaps *a* is receptually much more similar to *c* than to *b*; still, salience has the power to swing perceptual similarity the other way.

Psychologists ordinarily speak simply of the stimulus, where I am speaking of what is salient in the episode. One reason for my speaking this way is that there can be multiple salience, and in varying degrees, within an episode. In classical terms one would speak, in such a case, of simultaneous stimuli of unequal strengths. But the salience version suggests a field of gradations rather than just one or several clean-cut stimuli, and this I find good. Further, the salience version encourages us to think of the overall episode as basic, and to think of its operative components or features as abstracted from these episodes by the psychologist on the basis of collations of the subject's behavior.

Salience shows itself in behavior through the behavioral evidence for perceptual similarity. How salience is shown by perceptual similarity is evident from the above example of the cat. Talking of salience does, however, invite a convenient modicum of mentalistic idiom. The color of some object may be said to be salient in one episode, and the shape of the same object may be said to be salient in another episode. The color of the object is salient in the one episode because of its brilliance and saturation, and the shape is salient in the other episode because of boundary contrast or movement. It would be intolerable to deprive ourselves of these quick and vivid ways of speaking. But let us remember that this is all meant to be, in the end, a matter of physiological mechanisms, manifested in behavior.

We noted various conditions of salience: focal position, motion, brightness, boundary contrast, gaudy color. Salience can also be induced by the lingering traces of an earlier episode. The trace will tend to accentuate the similarity of that past episode to the present one by enhancing the salience of the features of the present episode in which that similarity resides. Thus it is that present salience is affected by past experience. The other conditions of salience just now listed are, in contrast, innate. It is as if, along with our acquired traces, we had a fund of innate traces that were inducing the salience of the bright colors and shape boundaries and the rest. It is as if there were racial memory—and indeed there is, if we choose to speak thus of natural selection.

The trace of a past episode fluctuates in vividness. Its vividness will depend partly on how similar that episode was to the present one and partly on the *strength* of the trace. By its strength I mean its capacity to be enlivened by present similarities. That strength will depend partly on recency; traces tend to wear out. But Freud has warned against overrating this tendency.

Between the trace of a past episode and the present episode, we see, the enlivening effect is reciprocal. Similarities enliven the trace; here is the familiar matter of our being reminded of the past episode by similarities in the present. And conversely, as just now stated, the trace enhances the salience of the present episode at its points of similarity to the past one. We can account in this way for the power that the sound of the word 'dog' has to draw our attention to a dog that we would otherwise have overlooked. The account is as follows: a trace survives of a past episode of impingement from which we learned the word; an episode, that, in which the creature was vividly seen and the word heard. The present episode of impingements resembles that one in part, namely in the sound of the word. Consequently the trace of the past episode enhances the salience of other points of resemblance, and lo the dog.

We tend to think of the enlivened trace of an ocular impingement as if it were itself a visual experience similar to what was occasioned by that impingement, only fainter: a visual image. There is even a certain aptness in so regarding it, on account of the effect of the trace upon salience. If we think of the enlivened trace as an image, then in the above example we can think of the enhanced salience of the dog as brought about by superposing the trace upon the otherwise inconspicuous real dog of the current scene. Likewise the power of verbal suggestion to induce visual illusion falls plausibly into place. This mentalistic angle could have heuristic value for the neurophysiologist, by suggesting that the neurophysiology of the trace may resemble the neurophysiology of the original sensation. This shared mechanism may someday be explained, just as the genes, posited at first as hypothetical bodies, were finally explained by molecular biology. We do well surely to avail ourselves of any such heuristic benefits of the mentalistic idiom, while keeping the dangers of an uncritical mentalism firmly in mind. I shall say more of this in §9.

§8. *Pleasure*

Foregoing sections have been lightly strewn with allusions in the classical idiom to the reinforcement and extinction of responses to stimuli. Certain deviant ways of speaking of these matters seem to offer advantages, but I am slow about edging over to them for fear of hindering communication.

Since §5 the polyadic relation of perceptual similarity has dominated the scene, as a relation among episodes in the subject's life. Each episode is brief, but it embraces everything that the subject is doing and suffering at the time. Any focus on special aspects of this broad cross section is the selective work of the relation of perceptual similarity. In §7, then, I invoked salience as a way of capturing or coagulating the product of this selective work on the part of perceptual similarity. Salience took on some of the burden ordinarily carried by the notion of stimulus. Now I shall propose a further shift of model or idiom, which tempers the classical polarity between stimulus and response. But the classical idiom has virtues of succinctness, and I shall still lapse into it from time to time.

Episodes are pleasant or unpleasant in varying degrees. It has already been explained that the strength of a trace varies with recency; also that the trace preserves information needed for perceptual similarity. I must now add that the strength of the trace varies also with the pleasure or discomfort of the episode, and that the trace preserves an index of pleasure or discomfort.[1] Where the trace is that of a pleasant episode, the subject is impelled so to exert himself as to increase the similarity of the present episode to that pleasant past one; and this drive will vary in strength with the vividness of the trace. Correspondingly, where the trace is that of an unpleasant episode, the subject is impelled to decrease the similarity or hinder its increase.

The drive to increase or decrease the similarity will therefore vary with the degree of pleasantness or unpleasantness of the earlier episode. This follows because the strength of the trace varies in that fashion, and its vividness varies with its strength (§7), and the drive with the vividness.

The drive will vary also with the degree of perceptual similarity that already obtains. This follows because the vividness of the trace varies in that fashion (§7) and the drive with the vividness. It is a convenient effect, for it sets the subject to trying to recapture pleasant episodes on which he already has a head start, or to avert unpleasant ones that have already begun to recur.

Learning, thus viewed, is a matter of learning to warp the trend of episodes, by intervention of one's own muscles, in such a way as to simulate a pleasant earlier episode. To learn is to learn to have fun. Behaviorally, the shoe is on the other foot: an episode counts as pleasant if, through whatever unidentified mechanism of nerves and hormones, it implants a drive to reproduce it. The pleasure is measured by the strength of this

1. See Young, p. 621, on mnemons.

drive. And all this applies also in reverse, to the avoiding of the unpleasant.

Thus consider the learning of the word 'red'. Suppose the child happens to utter the word in the course of the random babbling that is standard procedure in small children, and suppose a red ball happens to be conspicuously present at the time. The parent rewards the child, perhaps only by somehow manifesting approval. Thus in a certain brief minute in the history of overall impingements on the child's sensory surfaces there were these features among others: there were light rays in the red frequencies, there were sound waves in the air and in the child's headbones caused by the child's own utterance of the word 'red', there were the impacts on the proprioceptors of the child's tongue and larynx occasioned by that utterance, and there were the impacts, whatever they were, that made the episode pleasant. On a later occasion a red shawl is conspicuously present. Its color makes for a degree of perceptual similarity between the pleasant earlier episode and the present, thus enlivening the trace of that episode. The child contorts his speech muscles so as to add what more he can to the similarity: he again says 'red', and we may hope that the similarity is yet further enhanced by a recurrence of the reward.

Or take again the animal (§§1, 5). He had been through a pleasant episode whose salient features included the circular stripe, the pressing of the lever, and the emergence of food. His present episode is perceptually similar to that one to the extent of the circular stripe, or, what is fairly similar for him, the seven spots. He adds what more he can to the similarity by again pressing the lever.

Similarity is partial. As a history of variously similar episodes accumulates, the traces compete and determine the net resultant drive as by the adding of vectors, or composition of forces. Thus let us prolong the above example. The episode of the red shawl proved pleasant, like that of the red ball. But there was also an unfortunate episode of a yellow rose. This episode started out bearing little perceptual similarity to the two previous ones, but still the traces of those previous ones had their share of vividness simply because those episodes were so recent and pleasant. The two traces jointly proved sufficient to impel the child to recreate what he could of those episodes; so again he contributed the sound 'red', inducing that much present similarity to both of those past episodes. However, the further feature that had made those episodes pleasant was not forthcoming this time. On the contrary, this episode proved unpleasant: a window slammed. And now we move to yet another episode, in which the child is confronted with a red rose. Its color enlivens, through perceptual similarity, the traces of the pleasant episodes of the red ball and the red shawl; and its shape enlivens the trace of the unpleasant episode of the yellow rose. Will he say 'red'? To do so would increase the perceptual similarity of the present episode to that of the yellow flower; insofar as he is impelled not to. But it would increase the perceptual similarity to the two pleasant episodes, so the score is two to one in favor. He says it, and the story concludes on a happy note.

All this is of course easily enough described in classical terms of the reinforcement and inhibition of responses by conditioning. But a certain advantage of the present approach is suggested by the next example. Imagine a pleasant episode one of whose various salient features was the sound of the word 'preposterous' spoken by a parent. Later, prompted by the recurrence of some others of those conspicuous features, the child undertakes to enhance the overall similarity of the present episode to that pleasant one by sounding the word himself. Now the parent's saying 'preposterous' in the first episode belongs on the stimulus side, and the child's saying it in the second episode belongs on the response side. But by speaking of perceptual similarity of episodes as above, rather than in the polar terms of stimulus and response, we exploit the auditory similarity of the two utterances in the child's ear and abstract from their difference of source. There are many incidental differences anyway between any two episodes, and in the present case we are enabled to relegate the difference of speaker to this category. Radical separation of the stimulus and response would have obstructed this account.

People and other primates are inveterate imitators and imitatrices. We are said to have an instinct for imitation. I just now explained imitation in one instance, however, without special assumption. For the child would be said in this instance to have imitated the parent, not only in saying 'preposterous' but in saying it in circumstances similar to those in which the parent said it. Much else that goes by the name of imitation is perhaps similarly covered.

The child had of course already acquired the muscular techniques for producing desired sounds. Whereas perceptual similarity and the pleasure principle are concerned with motivation, this is the question of engineering. I shall not be concerned with it except to recognize its existence. How does the small child know which muscles to pull? It is the general question of acquiring muscular skills. We must recognize a disposition to make random movements in an experimental spirit. Infant babbling is an example. And we must assume some neural mechanism, of the nature of feedback, whereby practice makes perfect.[2]

Clearly pleasure is not constant under receptual similarity, nor under perceptual similarity. Episodes receptually or perceptually very similar to an episode *a* cannot be depended upon to be as much fun as *a*. For let us not forget the internal states. They are consequences largely of earlier episodes, and belong neither to current reception nor to current perception. We have been at pains to screen them out of any perceptual similarity comparisons. But they are part still of the episode *a*, and can contribute to its pleasure. The episode may be pleasant because of some idyllic memory that the subject was already entertaining at the time, or because of some uncommonly eupeptic phase in his digestive cycle. Later he will flex such muscles as are calculated to induce a perceptually similar episode, unrewarding though perceptual similarity may in this case be.[3] For that matter, he may also manage to flex again those unidentified little muscles, perhaps laryngeal among other, that went into the entertaining of the idyllic memory. Insofar, he is enhancing not just perceptual similarity but something more. (The eupeptic feature will have to go by the board, however, since the smooth musculature is beyond his control.)

Summed up, here is how action looks in terms of perceptual similarity and the pleasure principle. The subject basks in present impingements and puts his best foot forward. Traces of past

2. See Holt, Chapters VI-VIII, on the physiology of all this.

3. Herrnstein's theory of superstition fits in here.

episodes tell him what to seek and what to avoid. Similarities point his strategy, which is that of exploiting the head starts, improving the advantages. The inductive method is implicit in that strategy, for in effect that strategy consists in reproducing some components of a past episode in the hope that other components will accompany them, or in averting some components of a past episode for fear that others may accompany them.

This hedonistic model is of the kind that Troland (p. 278f) approvingly calls "hedonism of the past" and associates with Thorndike. Hedonistic theories of action have long had their distinguished champions and their distinguished critics. One counterargument is that pleasure, being mental, cannot move muscles. This point need not detain us, since pleasantness is for me an attribute of bodily episodes, manifested in behavior. There are plausible notions of its physiological mechanism; thus Holt (pp. 226, 232) pictures pleasantness and unpleasantness in terms of harmony and conflict of motor impulses.

A more serious objection to hedonism is simply that it is unrealistic as an account of responsible adult behavior. For instance my self-imposed activity, thinking and writing, is not fun. Very well; responsible adult behavior is an obscure and complicated matter. Still, when we are looking for the elements of the learning process at its simplest, perceptual similarity and the pleasure principle afford a reasonable schema.

part II
breaking into language

§9. *Mentalism and language*

The mentalistic idiom is at the tip of one's tongue. In treating of perceptual similarity I have stressed behavior, but the term has strong overtones of introspection. In talking of the learning process we commonly deal in mentalistic terms of induction and expectation. The animal confronted with the seven spots may be said to expect the lever to deliver a pellet and not a shock, and he may be said to have reached this expectation by induction from past episodes.

The talk of a pleasure principle was a conspicuous instance of mentalistic idiom, however behavioral the intent. Similarly for salience and traces. And we even found heuristic value in thinking of activated traces as images (§7).

Mentalism thus has its uses as a stimulant. Like other stimulants, it should be used with caution. Mental entities are unobjectionable if conceived as hypothetical physical mechanisms and posited with a view strictly to the systematizing of physical phenomena. They should be posited in the hope of their submitting someday to a full physical explanation in turn. Any vaguenesses or complexities that might obstruct that objective should be minimized. One must not mistake the familiarity of mentalistic talk for clarity, and thus be tempted into a dream world of introspection. Philosophers and Titchener-type psychologists have worried about whether one's triangle image is equilateral or scalene or oscillatory among various angularities. Some have wondered whether one's image of a speckled hen had an odd or an even number of spots or perhaps neither, and, if neither, how a number could be neither odd nor even. If we think of images aseptically as hypothetical neural states, these queer problems do not arise. A triangle image or a speckled-hen image is a neural state that requires no commitment to angle ratios or speck numbers.

Images, traditionally, were ideas. They were the least tenuous of the ideas (apart from sensations themselves), and hence the more insidious in luring the unwary farther into that misty realm. Berkeley and Hume were wary; they even drew the line at the abstract triangle idea, admitting images of the specific triangular shapes only. At any rate it is the facile resort to ideas in general, not just images, that renders the mentalistic idiom disastrous. Questions of the mechanics of learning subside into idle questions of the causal connections of ideas. An illusion of understanding is created by pushing the problems back into a realm that is too dim for their easy detection.

Our dissociation from the old epistemologists has brought both freedom and responsibility. We gain access to the resources of natural science and we accept the methodological restraints of natural science. In our account of how science might be acquired we do not try to justify science by some prior and firmer philosophy, but neither are we to maintain less than scientific standards. Evidence must regularly be sought in external objects, out where observers can jointly observe it. Speculation is allowable if recognized for what it is and conducted with a view to the possible access of evidence at some future stage. C. S. Peirce has well stated that "the only way of investigating a psychological question is by inference from external facts" (5.249).

We want to know how men can have achieved the conjectures and abstractions that go into scientific theory. How can we pursue such an inquiry while talking of external things to the exclusion of ideas and concepts? There is a way: we can talk of language. We can talk of concrete men and their concrete noises. Ideas are as may be, but the words are out where we can see and hear them. And scientific theories, however speculative and however abstract, are in words. One and the same theory can be expressed in different words, so people say, but all can perhaps agree that there are no theories apart from words. Or, if there are, there is little to be lost in passing over them.

In turning away from the ideas and looking to the words, we are taking the nominalist strategy. Perversely, there persists an old and stubborn tendency of the opposite kind: to appeal to the ideas when theorizing about the words. Language, we are told, serves to convey ideas. When we learn language we learn to associate its words with the same ideas with which other speakers associate them. Now how do we know that these ideas are the same? And, so far as communication is concerned, who cares? We have all learned to apply the word 'red' to blood, tomatoes, ripe apples, and boiled lobsters. The associated idea, the associated sensation, is as may be. Language bypasses the idea and homes on the object. Than the idea there is little less useful to the study of language.

Infant learning is a bright domain, and there behavioristic psychology blooms. The beginnings of language are learned ostensively. The needed stimuli are right out there in front, and mystery is at a minimum. The old-time talk of ideas, ideas grasped and ideas conveyed, is given up without a wrench. Subtleties and obscurities crowd in, however, when we press to less primitive levels of language learning. The child learns to recombine his growing vocabulary into new sentences of his own and to use them properly. Up to a point, this process in turn stands fairly well to reason. The child learns some brief sentences as wholes in the obvious way, by hearing them from adults in the appropriate observable circumstances; and then he makes new ones by analogical substitution, supplanting a component word of an acquired sentence by some other word of his acquired vocabulary. Soon, though, his learning process becomes much harder to picture and to conjecture about. He gets to producing sentences that bear no important relation to concurrent observable circumstances at all. He utters sentences about the past and the future—sentences whose only connection with present circumstances is that they are triggered by someone's present remark. In the fullness of time he gets to producing sentences that bear no very clear relation even to observable circumstances in the past or future; sentences, these, of myth or theory or conjecture. The best of these sentences do enjoy some kind of connection still with observation, but the philosophers who devote themselves to the logic and methodology of science have been hard put to it to say in explicit detail just what the appropriate connections might be.

It is proverbial, or used to be, that man in his study of nature falls back on the old-time religion to fill in where his scientific explanations leave off. It is at least equally true that man in his study of language falls back on the old-time mentalistic semantics to fill in where his scientific explanations leave off. Mentalism, supernaturalism, and other unwholesome cultures thrive in dark places.

A healthy suspicion has been getting around that the idea idea is not quite respectable, and for this reason it is tending to exert its power less overtly than it did in the days of Kant, Hume, and Locke. It is still ill concealed, certainly, under the name of proposition; for a proposition, when not taken as a mere sentence, is the idea that a sentence expresses. Happily there is an increasing tendency to be guarded in one's talk of propositions.

However, a philosopher who is chary of talking of ideas and propositions is apt still to talk as blithely as a layman on the subject of translation. He tends uncritically to accept the relation of a sentence to its translation, as a relation that is intelligible outright. He thinks it makes sense to ask, of just about any sentence in any language, for an English translation. When I try to picture his uncritical acceptance of this relation, I can picture it only as an unconscious old-fashioned acceptance of the idea idea: one sentence is a translation of another if it expresses the same idea, the same thought, the same meaning, the same proposition.

What is wanted for a better understanding of the mechanics of language and language learning is a continuing adherence to externals. Conjectures about internal mechanisms are laudable insofar as there is hope of their being supported by neurological findings. But the idea idea of our fathers will be only in the way.

§10. *Observation sentences*

Midway in the preceding section we concluded that to account for man's mastery of scientific theory we should see how he acquires theoretical language. Our reason was that we can study words more responsibly than ideas. There is also a second reason, having to do with the relation between a scientific theory and the observations that support it. For this relation has, besides its epistemological aspect, a semantical aspect. Besides being the relation through which the sentences affirmed in the theory gain their support, it is the relation through which they gain their meaning. For we learn the language by relating its terms to the observations that elicit them. Now this learning process is a matter of fact, accessible to empirical science. By exploring it, science can in effect explore the evidential relation between science itself and its supporting observations.

The reason for the basic role of observations, both in the support of theory and in the learning of language, is their intersubjective immediacy. They are what witnesses will agree about, on the spot. They are the common ground on which to meet when there is disagreement. Hence their basic role in the support of theory. And in their intersubjective immediacy they are basic also to language learning, because we learn the language from other people in shared circumstances. Though we learn it largely by learning to relate strings of words to strings of words, somewhere there have to be nonverbal reference points, nonverbal circumstances that can be intersubjectively appreciated and associated with the appropriate utterance on the spot. Ostensive learning is fundamental, and requires observability. The child and the parent must both see red when the child learns 'red', and one of them must see also that the other sees red at the time.

The two roles of observations, their role in the support of theory and their role in the learning of language, are inseparable. Observations are relevant as evidence for the support of theory because of those very associations, between observable events and theoretical vocabulary, whereby we learn the theoretical vocabulary in the first place. Hence, of course, the commonplaces of the verification theory of meaning. The meaning of a sentence lies in the observations that would support or refute it. To learn a language is to learn the meaning of its sentences, and hence to learn what observations to count as evidence for and against them. The evidence relation and the semantical relation of observation to theory are coextensive.

But the old champions of a verification theory of meaning went wrong in speaking too blithely of the meaning of individual sentences. Most sentences do not admit separately of observational evidence. Sentences interlock. An observation may refute some chunk of theory comprising a cluster of sentences, and still leave us free to choose which of the component sentences to continue to count as true and which to abandon. The evidence relation is thus intricate and indirect. The same, of course, is true of the semantical relation. The semantical relation of observation to the theoretical language is similarly intricate and indirect, since we learn the language only partly by associating terms or sentences directly with observation, and partly by linking them to one another. The evidence relation, in all its intricacy, and the semantical relation, in all its intricacy, are coextensive still.

Let us now come more nearly to grips with these matters. What are observations? They are visual, auditory, tactual, olfactory. They are sensory, evidently, and thus subjective. Yet it was crucial to the use of observations, both as evidence and as semantical reference points, that they be socially shared. Should we say then that the observation is not the sensation after all, but the shared environmental circumstances? No, for there is no presumption of intersubjective agreement about the environing situation either; two men will assess it differently, partly because of noticing different features and partly because of entertaining different theories.

There is a way out of this difficulty over the notion of observation. It consists in talking neither of sensation nor of environing situation, but of language: talking of language at the observational end no less than at the theoretical end. I do not suggest that observations themselves are something verbal, but I propose that we drop the talk of observation and talk instead of observation sentences, the sentences that are said to report observations: sentences like 'This is red', 'This is a rabbit'. No matter that sensations are private, and no matter that men may take radically different views of the environing situation; the observation *sentence* serves nicely to pick out what witnesses can agree on.

Since I propose to dodge the problem of defining observation by talking instead of observation sentences, I had better not define observation sentences as sentences that report observations. Nor do I need to. The requirement of intersubjective agreement already affords us just the definition we need. A sentence is observational insofar as its truth value, on any occasion, would be agreed to by just about any member of the speech community witnessing the occasion. This definition depends still on the idea of membership in the speech community, but that presents no problem; we can recognize membership in the speech community by mere fluency of dialogue, something we can witness even without knowing the language.

We might want to hedge our definition of observation sentence a little, so as not to count as observation sentences those platitudes on which all speakers will agree come what may. Such sentences, which I call "stimulus-analytic" (§21), can be eliminated by requiring that an observation sentence be an *occasion* sentence, that is, a sentence that does not command assent or dissent once and for all, but only variably from occasion to occasion. However, these are uninteresting legalisms. What is worth noticing is that we have here a behavioral criterion of what to count as an observation sentence. It does not appeal to sense data or other epistemological preconceptions.

We noticed earlier, when talking vaguely still of observations rather than observation sentences, that the ability of witnesses to agree in their observations was crucial on two counts. It was necessary for evidential purposes, as providing common ground on which to meet when there is disagreement about theory. And it was necessary for semantical purposes, as enabling our elders to assess the appropriateness of the occasions with which we were associating our newly acquired words and sentences. Such, then, are the two crucial roles of observation sentences: evidential and semantical. Observation sentences are sentences on which scientists can reach agreement when they are trying to reconcile their theories, and they are sentences that can be socially checked against their occasions of utterance when we are picking up a language. Because of this semantical trait of observation sentences it is they that are learned most readily, affording the entering wedge in the acquisition of one's language. Observation sentences are the gateway to language, as to science.

Typical observation sentences are 'Red' (or 'This is red', 'I see red'), 'Rabbit', 'It is raining'. Mostly they treat not of sensations but of external things, since they admit of public verification. Their distinctive trait is the sufficiency of present impingements.

To appreciate the sense in which we may say that present impingements suffice for observation sentences, consider sentences of the other sort: a remark about ancient Egypt or the nucleus of the atom or the destiny of man. Now it must be granted that these latter sentences also are triggered by present impingements: perhaps by the sight of a page or a bas relief or a photographic plate or someone's question. And it must be granted, conversely, that one's readiness even to affirm or assent to an observation sentence—'It is raining', 'This is red', 'That is a rabbit'—is dependent still on one's earlier training, one's rudimentary language learning. But we know the social criterion that distinguishes the two sorts of sentences. If the remark about ancient Egypt is put as a question to two fluent speakers in the presence of impingements as nearly alike as you please, one speaker may assent and the other may not. Similarly for the remark about the nucleus of the atom, or about human destiny. But you will get like verdicts if in the presence of the same impingements you query an observation sentence.

There has been a tendency in recent philosophy to question the notion of observation, or of observation sentence. One complaint is much the same as the Gestalt psychologist's objection to sensory atomism (§1); viz., the ubiquity of unconscious inference. But observation sentences in the present sense are not open to that objection, for they are not about sense data.

A second complaint is that what count as observations for the specialist often do not count as such for the layman. An answer to this objection is that the notion of observation sentence is relative to a linguistic community. If a sentence would qualify as an observation sentence for the scientist and not for the layman, it is couched in a technical sublanguage in which the layman is not a fluent communicant. A better answer is to insist on adhering to the broad linguistic community for the philosophical criterion, thus not counting the specialist's recondite sentence as an observation sentence in the strict sense. For the specialist can always be driven back to the less technical levels of evidence, though in practice he cites only what is needed for reassuring his trained colleagues.

A third complaint is that no datum is wholly safe from repudiation, if it conflicts with a theory that has overwhelming support from other quarters. Now we can accept this point as true but not as an objection. Our definition of observation sentence speaks only of concurrence of present witnesses, and sets no bar to subsequent retractions.

The definition does raise a subtler problem, however—a problem that was already noted in another connection in §6. The definition speaks of joint witnessing. In a more precise statement, it would speak of witnesses subject to receptually similar impingements; and thus it would raise again the homology question that we noted at the end of §6.

Still, the definition is as sharp as the notions of witness and linguistic community on which it depends. It is good as behavioral concepts go.

§11. *Ostensive learning*

Observation sentences are the gateway to language. We can learn them first because we have only to key them to current episodes; there is no *arrière pensée,* no need of deduction or theorizing, no searching of memory. This is because other speakers, whom we imitate and who encourage our own behavior, have associated the sentences with those same ranges of concurrent impingement. Not that each of us learns all his observation sentences by direct conditioning in this way. Each of us happens to learn many observation sentences in indirect ways, by verbal explanation or by verbal context or by analogical construction from component words previously learned. Some of us master a particular observation sentence in one way, some in another. Still, an observation sentence is one that *can* be learned by direct conditioning. It is within the scope of standard animal training.

Other sentences, not observational, can be *partially* learned by that same direct conditioning. The child can learn 'flimsy', or 'It is flimsy', ostensively from conspicuous instances, and may wrongly treat it as observational for a while, thus withholding it from things not visibly flimsy. When fully mastered, 'flimsy' fails the test of observationality because of covert flimsiness. A contrivance may be declared flimsy on sight by one observer and not by another, according to prior experience with things of the same make. 'Sick' is another example: there are the patently sick and there are those who are sick only to the trained eye.

The term 'red', functioning as a one-word sentence, is an observation sentence that already figured conspicuously in illustrations of the learning process in §5 and §8. Mentalistically described, the child's learning of this sentence consists in his proceeding inductively from observation and experiment to a general unspoken knowledge of the circumstances in which to expect adults to assent to 'red'. Described in passive and less septic terms, he is being trained by successive reinforcements and extinctions to say 'red' on the right occasions and those only. He exerts himself to enhance the overall similarity of present impingements to pleasant past episodes that included the sound 'red' and to diminish similarity to unpleasant episodes that included that sound.

The child's success in learning this and other observation sentences depends on substantial agreement between his similarity standards and those of the adult. For he is anticipating the adult's reactions by extrapolating from past samples according to his own similarity standards. Clearly, therefore, the similarity concerned here is perceptual similarity, that being fairly uniform over society. The child may make some wrong extrapolations because of random interferences from his flux of inner states, but these wrong tries will be extinguished as the conditioning goes on.

In §6 we considered how to isolate pure perceptual similarity, screening out the interferences from within. Aid is now visible from the side of language: perceptual similarity relates the episodes that warrant assent to an observation sentence.

The learning of an observation sentence amounts to determining, as we may say, its *similarity basis*. By this I mean the distinctive trait shared by the episodes appropriate to that observation sentence; the shared trait in which their perceptual similarity consists. In learning the sentence the child may approximate its similarity basis little by little. In learning 'red' he has to learn that it is a question of sight, not some other sense. He has to find the proper direction in the scene, and how much to count: how big a patch. He has to learn what aspect of the patch to count; he might think that what mattered in his first red patch was the shape and not the color. Also there is the question of chromatic latitude: how orange can red get? Having been rewarded for saying 'red' on one exposure, he can only conjecture what similarity might warrant saying it again. We may expect him to have to make a number of trials and eliminate a number of errors before he is shunted onto the right track for good.

Chromatic latitude is the worst of it. Similarity by the child's innate lights ascends the spectrum in an unbroken chain, and red dwindles only by a gradual diminution of reinforcement on the part of society. Some portions of the spectrum show steeper subjective gradations than others, perhaps, but there are no natural segments, as witness the different segmentations of color nomenclature in different societies.[1]

The other matters that the child needed to learn about the similarity basis of the word 'red' could in principle be left to long-term inductive resolution, like the indeterminacy of how far up

1. Cf. Lenneberg and Roberts.

the spectrum to apply 'red'. Among the myriad features of episodes of overall impingement, those features that are irrelevant to 'red' would in the long run cease to compete. Times when the sound 'red' was reinforced would show their common features ever more clearly as their irrelevant features continued to vary at random, until at last the child—mentally a child still, if physically well along in years—would get to using the word 'red' at just the right times. In practice, of course, things move faster, thanks to salience. No multiple inductive steps are needed to eliminate from competition all features of the original scene outside the relevant color patch itself, if that patch is set off in any of various effective ways: focally situated, brightly lighted, garishly colored, emphatically outlined, moving against a background. Or, again, the child would be spared the mistake of extrapolating on the basis of shape if on first exposure the red happened to be bright and its boundaries vague.

Salience thus expedites the learning of observation words exceedingly. Here it is that *pointing* confers its benefits. The scene is selectively enlivened by the conspicuous intrusion of a finger in the foreground of a chosen object, or by the motion of a finger outlining a chosen region.

Wittgenstein noted some perplexities of pointing.[2] How do we know how much or what aspect of the ostended region is intended? How do we even recognize pointing as pointing? How do we know that an ostensively defined term is not a term for the pointing finger? How do you ostend ostension? Well, mistakes do occur. The indri, a lemur of Madagascar, owes this name to a Malagasy expression meaning "There it goes." The French naturalist Pierre Sonnerat supposed at the time that the ostending native was naming the animal.[3] Still, ostension is brought under control on the whole; and let us think how. Pointing, we saw, contributes by heightening the salience of a portion of the visual field. Primitively this salience is conferred on the pointing finger and its immediate background and neighborhood indiscriminately, through the familiar agency of movement and

2. Paragraphs 33-38, 454.

3. American Heritage Dictionary; reference courtesy of David K. Lewis. Also Encyclopedia Britannica, 1911.

contrast. Even in this primitive effect there is a gain: most of the irrelevant stretches of the scene are eliminated from attention, and much laborious elimination by induction is thus averted. Some limited induction may remain to be done, some reinforcement of the verbal response in the absence of the pointing finger and some extinction of it in the presence of the pointing finger, before the subject succeeds in eliminating the pointing finger in favor of the thing or feature for which the word is intended. In later cases we skip even this limited bit of fumbling, having learned the pointing custom.

§12. *Assent*

Pointing, we see, serves to expedite the learning of terms that might otherwise be learned only through a long sifting of similarities and differences of overall impingement patterns. Now another device that greatly expedites such learning is *assent*. Certainly assent and dissent must very soon supplant the routine of saying 'red' in a red presence and being rewarded. If the child were to persist in volunteering the names of passing colors and other observables, he would soon bore his purveyor of rewards beyond the point of diminishing returns. Increasingly the child contents himself with answering 'yes' and 'no' when asked, and with asking and taking 'yes' and 'no' as answers. In the continuing enterprise of ostensive learning, these two vocables are the laconic refrain.

I have made much of the learning of 'red' because it was easy to talk about, and it was for the same reason that I have dwelt on that aspect of the learning of 'red' that consists in learning to volunteer the word in the presence of red. If this emphasis has given a distorted impression of the early phases of language learning, the reflections on assent to which we are now turning will help to redress the balance.

To begin with, it would be wrong to suppose that learning when to volunteer statements of fact *or* to assent to them is all or most of what goes into language learning. Learning to react in appropriate nonverbal ways to heard language is equally important. The child learns to react appropriately to many words before being moved to volunteer them. Dogs learn to act appropriately on some words without learning to volunteer any. Much of what is earliest and most urgent in language learning, furthermore, is a matter of neither stating nor assenting nor acting upon statements, but of importuning.

But statement learning is what is relevant to our study, which aims at understanding the acquisition of scientific theory. As for concentrating on the child's statements rather than his nonverbal responses to statements, this is a clear matter of strategy; verbal behavior can be more handily classified than the other, and we can get whatever we need by probing from this side. And note by the way that though the child learns most of language by hearing the adults and emulating them, his very ability to imitate is accounted for (if §8 is right) by the more basic mechanisms that have been our concern.

We must by all means examine the learning of assent, for this device is indispensable to a child's progress in the art of statement. The child must learn how and when to assent to parents' queries, as lately remarked, because of the parents' limited tolerance of childish initiative. Conversely, the child who has reached the point of wanting to verify and improve his own usage must learn to query statements for parents' assent; for the utterances volunteered by the parents are too sporadic to meet his needs. These are two reasons why assent is indispensable, and a firmer reason still can be added. For there are observation sentences whose proper occasions of use cannot be discovered by mere watchful waiting even with the best of luck; they can only be checked by query and assent. I refer to observation sentences with overlapping ranges. By just passively noting the episodes of impingement in which one's elders volunteered 'rabbit' or 'animal', one would have no way of making sure that all the things cited as rabbits would count also as animals, or whether any of the things cited as animals might count also as rabbits. By query and assent, on the other hand, it is the work of a moment.

It is worth noting, in passing, that the method of query and assent is indispensable likewise, and for the same reasons, to the field linguist who is breaking into an unknown language by investigating native speakers. At first there is little he can do but watch and wait; but his progress will be slight until he has noted and guessed enough to enable him to start volunteering native words or observation sentences on his own and querying them for assent. It is the indispensable means of tapping the reservoir of linguistic dispositions. A native sign of assent is apt to be recognizable by this obvious partial criterion: a speaker will assent to a sentence, if queried, in circumstances sufficiently similar to those in which he volunteers the sentence. (For the meaning of 'sufficiently' see §5 on neighborhoods.) Firmer control can be gained by finding also what might plausibly be taken as a sign of dissent; and the partial criterion for this is that a speaker will dissent in no circumstances sufficiently similar to those in which he volunteers the sentence. Troubles will be compounded, of course, if the sentences tried happen not to be observation sentences and hence not to be linked to concurrent circumstances. But one does what one can.

Let us return then to home ground and consider how our child might get on to the trick of assent. The mechanism of perceptual similarity and the pleasure principle proves to cover the case quite well. One of the child's rewarding episodes may be supposed to have included a conspicuous show of red together with the sound 'red' from his own mouth, followed by the sound 'yes' from the parent. In a later episode there is again the color and again the sound 'red'. Such is the partial similarity of the later episode to the earlier. There are of course incidental differences, and one of these just happens to be that the sound 'red' issued from the parent this time, actually with interrogative intent. Anyway the child is moved as usual to heighten the resemblance, so he supplies another element of the earlier episode, the sound 'yes'. Rewarded again, he has learned to say 'yes' in the presence of the color red and the sound 'red'. Unpleasant episodes will discourage him from saying 'yes' when he hears the sound 'red' in the absence of the color.

In this account we see again an advantage of thinking in terms of perceptual similarity and the pleasure principle rather than in the polar terms of stimulus and response. It is the same advantage that was seen in the treatment of imitation (§8). For note that 'red' is spoken by the child and 'yes' by the parent in the first episode and vice versa in the second.

We have imagined how the child might learn to assent to the specific observation sentence 'red'. He would learn similarly to assent to other queried observation sentences, one by one, as readily as to 'red'. Soon he would learn the general trick of assenting when an observation sentence previously learned is queried for the first time. He would learn this by generalizing from a few cases that he had learned separately in the way in which we imagined him to learn to assent to 'red'. But now what might the method or mechanism of such generalization be?

It is here, I think, that we must appeal to the *language-dependent* learning of language: to learning that depends on other locutions previously learned. What is learned here, in particular, is an equivalence: assent to a sentence entails the same rewards or penalties as a repetition of the sentence would entail. This learning depends, like other learning, on an appreciation of similarity; but this time it is a language-dependent similarity. The shared feature in which the similarity lies is perhaps an introspective sense of willingness to repeat the heard sentence; a sense of freedom from inhibition. In venturing to speculate thus on inward sense I relax my behaviorism, but not much; I speak only of an incipient drive toward overt behavior.

The child's learning of dissent would not begin in quite the way in which we imagined his learning of assent to have begun. That began with his learning to assent to a specific sentence, 'red'. His learning of this depended on a rewarding episode in which he said 'red' and the parent said 'yes'. If we try a parallel account of dissent, the trouble is that an episode in which the child said 'red' and the parent said 'no' would tend not to have been a rewarding one which the child would try to recreate. If by chance the child babbled 'no' when the parent said 'red' in the absence of the color, then indeed he would be rewarded and would have his start; but this line is too improbable. We can perhaps more easily suppose that the child eventually achieves a general second-order learning of dissent without having first learned to dissent to various specific observation sentences independently. Mastery of assent could be a helpful preliminary step to this general mastery of dissent. Moving from the one to the other is a matter of coming to appreciate that dissent is rewarded where assent is penalized and vice versa. If the shared feature underlying the general mastery of assent was a sense of willingness to repeat the heard sentence, a sense of freedom from inhibition, then the feature underlying the general mastery of dissent is simply the sense of inhibition.

§13. *Values*

Scientific theory stands proudly and notoriously aloof from value judgments. Let us look briefly into this relation, or want of relation, from the point of view of language learning. At first let us concentrate on 'good' as applied to things to eat.

Without doubt the term is learned at first on a par with observation terms such as 'red'.[1] The child learns perhaps to assent to it in the presence of toffee. A little subsequent trial and error shunts him off the wrong similarity dimensions, such as stickiness, and settles him properly on pleasure as the feature shared by good episodes. It is a curious case of convergence of factors. The two factors that make for learning, in general, are perceptual similarity and the pleasure principle; but in this case pleasure does double duty, serving also as the similarity basis. The similarity basis and the reinforcement coincide here. Under such auspices the term 'good' must come through as a red-letter word indeed.

In §11 we noted 'flimsy' and 'sick' as terms that could be partly learned by ostension but did not qualify as observation terms. We noted that the child might even misuse such terms as observational at first, by dissenting from their application to covert cases instead of properly withholding his verdict. We noted that in adult usage these terms fail of observationality according to our criterion; observers may differ in their verdicts to 'flimsy' or 'sick' on present evidence because of different past experience.

1. "Good and bad," Peirce wrote (5.247), "are feelings which first arise as predicates."

Now the term 'good' turns out somewhat similarly: tasters give different verdicts, differing as they do in what they like. The child gets his good start on 'good', as on 'flimsy', from cases where there is general agreement; we *all* like toffee.[2] Later, failures of unanimity force him to have second thoughts on 'good(-tasting)' as on 'flimsy'.

But these second thoughts take different lines. In the case of 'flimsy' and 'sick' there are, he finds, ways of resolving the disagreements by pressing an investigation. These are terms of scientific theory, and evidence for their application can be marshalled that leads back to really observational terms. With 'good', said of taste, the case is otherwise; the disagreements are a dead end. *De gustibus non disputandum est.*

The above reflections on goodness of flavor clearly apply equally to the aesthetic good generally. What is perhaps less obvious, they apply in considerable part to the moral good as well. The child's early acts of obedience are agreeably rewarded and his early transgressions are spanked down. Thus we find the same convergence of factors here as before: the similarity basis of the term 'good', morally applied, is the reward itself. Obedience brings pleasure much as toffee does. The likening of obedience to toffee is indeed the very strategy of the parent's training program.

Introspection would have inclined me to expect that the 'good' of pleasure and the 'good' of righteousness were the merest homonyms, independently learned and calling perhaps for quite heteronymous translations in various other languages. But not so; their similarity bases are essentially one and the same, and most strikingly. The child can, however, easily learn a subordinate distinction between the aesthetic good and the moral good, between the tasty and the virtuous. For, within the broad similarity that relates all reinforcements, there is a sensible difference between those sensory inpingements that taste or feel good and those that herald what tastes or feels good. The difference grows, in the fullness of time, through failures in the heralding; virtue sometimes fails, I regret to say, to be rewarded.

2. W. S. Gilbert.

At this point it is anybody's guess whether the child will readjust his usage of the term 'good', through failure of expected reinforcements. Some children turn out one way and some, I regret to say, another.

It is one thing to learn the difference between right and wrong, and another thing to suit the action to the word. The one is a matter of learning good English, learning to talk; the other is a matter of learning good manners, learning to behave. The similarity basis for learning the word 'good' is reward, or impunity, and the basis of the moral training is the same, but still the lessons learned are different. The child may go on properly applying the word 'good' even after the training has stopped and the similarity basis has thus left off; for by then he has learned by enumeration what acts are called good by the linguistic community. Language confers its benefits through conformity of speech habits, and the individual stands to gain nothing from private linguistic deviation, however covert. But he may stand to gain much from wicked behavior, once the sanctions are dropped. It is remarkable how successful we often are in training the young to police themselves against their own selfish interests; surely there is a native amenability at the bottom of it all, and it has been favored by natural selection because of its survival value for the race taken collectively. But this is not language learning.

On the side of language learning we found that the 'good' of aesthetics and the 'good' of ethics began together. We saw further how the 'good' of aesthetics would subsequently distinguish itself both from observation terms and from terms of theoretical science. It differed from observation terms in that people disagree as to what tastes or looks good, and it differed from scientific terms in that there is no disputing about taste. Now on these counts the moral 'good' turns out quite otherwise. Normally and typically there is agreement in the community as to what to count as morally good; for morality, like language itself, is a community matter.

I think that what sets morals apart from scientific theory is a substantive point of modern scientific theory itself: a scientific doctrine as to the origins and basis of morality. Science sees the moral law no longer as coeval with the cosmos, but as the work of society. Therefore science addresses itself to the origins of the moral law, among other things, but does not incorporate its content. This divorce of science from moral values is a sophisticated manifestation, reflecting no significant quirk in language learning.

§14. *Masses and bodies*

'Red' is at once a term and a sentence. In past pages I treated it under the head of sentences—observation sentences—along with 'It is raining', because we were concerned with affirmation and assent. When we speak of it rather as a term, we are foreseeing its eventual use within longer sentences as a word naming or describing objects: describing bodies or surfaces or naming a color. Since my final concern in this book is with objective reference, I shall speak of 'red' and similar words mostly hereafter as terms, observation terms, rather than as sentences.

Much of what I said of 'red' in foregoing pages could be said equally of proper names of bodies, e.g. 'Mama', 'Fido', 'Jumbo'. For such names to qualify as observation terms, under my definition, we must indeed narrow the linguistic community to those who know these individuals by name. Let us do so, since such names belong with observation terms for purposes of the theory of learning.

Much of what I said of 'red' could be said also of mass terms such as 'sugar' and 'water'. The significant thing about a mass term is that it is closed with respect to aggregation. Two squares do not together constitute a square, nor two apples an apple; but when you add sugar to sugar the total is still sugar. On this score, color words like 'red' behave like mass terms. From the point of view of learning, moreover, these are all substantially alike, and like 'Mama' and 'Fido' as well. They all are observation terms, capable of being learned ostensively, and in each case to have learned the term is to have learned when to assent to it or dissent from it as an occasion sentence. Mama and water are very unlike, but to learn either term is to learn by induction the appropriate similarity basis. Mama, water, and red are recognizably recurring presences. Mama differs from water and red in being, for all her sporadic comings and goings, spatiotemporally continuous; but this is a sophisticated matter of physical theory with little bearing on the learning of observation terms.

Between Mama on the one hand and water or sugar or red on the other there are indeed differences, significant even at the level of ostensive learning. Sugar can be present in simultaneous separate portions; so can water; and so can red. Mama, on the other hand, when present at all, is visibly continuous, unless partially eclipsed by intervening bodies. And these casual eclipses offer little threat to Mama's integrity as a single Gestalt; for they are fleeting and they are independent of Mama's movements, responding rather with parallax to the movements of the observer.

Another difference between Mama and the masses is that the masses are amorphous. The similarity basis of the mass term 'sugar', or 'water', or 'red', has nothing to do with shape. On the other hand the similarity that links the various presentations of Mama is very much a matter of shape. Her visual shapes are many in the course of her various orientations and contortions, but they are joined by observed continuity of deformation. We do not keep Mama under observation, but we do watch her often enough as she changes visual shape in our field. The similarity that links the many presentations of Mama for us under the one name is not just static visual similarity, but a similarity that depends also on continuity of deformation and displacement. We may next recognize Mama because our new glimpse is visually similar to some earlier view that observably evolved from attested views by continuous deformation. Chains of such links are what hold Mama together.

I suggested that ostensive gestures do their work by heightening salience. A sweeping gesture of ostension can serve to heighten Mama's salience by following her through a characteristic brief episode of continuous deformation. Dynamic gestures serve nicely to differentiate the use of two terms by directing the salience differently through time. Ostension accompanied by utterance of 'Mama' continues to follow Mama after she casts off her red shawl; ostension accompanied by utterance of 'red' takes the other turning, following the shawl.

The similarity basis of 'Mama' was rather a long story. Each view of her is a continuous patch? Not quite; there was the little matter of eclipse and parallax. Each view of her is similarly shaped? No indeed, but there is the continuity of deformation. This rather tortuous sort of similarity is the unifying principle not only of Mama but of Fido and indeed of bodies generally. For all its tortuousness, it is apparently a sort of similarity that we are innately predisposed to appreciate. The well-known Gestalt effect is basic: the readiness to recognize a simple and unified figure, ignoring interruptions of outline. A similar readiness to recognize the persistence of an object in uniform motion, despite temporal interruption, is reported in early infancy: the baby will see an object pass behind a screen and show surprise when it does not duly emerge at the other side.[1] It is no wonder that bodies, bodily identity and bodily persistence, are the mainstay of ontology. Bodies, for the common man, are basically what there are; and even for the esoteric ontologist bodies are the point of departure. Man is a body-minded animal, among body-minded animals. Man and other animals are body-minded by natural selection; for body-mindedness has evident survival value in town and jungle.

I see little point, now or later, in trying to make the notion of body precise. Bodies are things like Mama and Fido and other animals, also apples, cups, chairs. The considerations that associate the presentations of Mama are what make for a body at this stage of our speculations: there is her synchronic visible continuity, interrupted only casually by partial eclipses, and there is her diachronic continuity of displacement and deformation. When the time comes for the precision of physical science, the notion of body can give way to the more inclusive, more recondite, and more precise notion of *physical object*. Any arbitrary congeries of particle-stages, however spatiotemporally gerrymandered or disperse, can count as a physical object. More of this in §§23, 34.

1. See Bower.

§15. *Individuation of bodies*

Mama is a body; red and water are not. This is no small difference. Still, all three terms share a certain semantic simplicity when contrasted with terms like 'dog'. We have learned those three terms insofar as we are able merely to tell whether Mama, red, and water are present, or salient in the scene. To learn 'dog' we have to learn more than presence. We have to learn also the individuative force of the term, the division of reference. We have to learn what to count as one dog and what to count as another.

In one way, 'dog' is like 'red' and 'water' and unlike 'Mama'. Red and water can come in simultaneous scattered portions. Similarly we can be confronted by many dogs at once. Mama is radically different; she comes at any one time as a single Gestalt, even if subject fleetingly to partial eclipses. But on this score 'dog' resembles also 'Mama' in a way: *each* dog comes at any one time as a single Gestalt. Also each dog resembles Mama in what counts for its unification over time; namely, continuity of displacement, continuity of visual distortion, continuity of discoloration. Each dog, like Mama, is a body.

We reflected that these body-unifying considerations, though complex, are rooted in instinct. Often they are enough to assure the right extrapolation from a single ostension. But not always. We saw how Mama and her red shawl could part company, and thereupon a continuing ostension could take either of two courses according as 'Mama' or 'red' was the word to be explained. Likewise in the case of the dogs, then, let us be prepared for dynamic ostensions of some duration.

Pleonasms are helpful in prolonging the ostension: we accompany the continuous gesture with not just the word 'dog', however slowly spoken, but with the pleonastic elaboration 'This is a dog'. A more extravagant pleonasm may come into play for purposes of further prolongation: we may say 'This is the same dog as this'.

The great difference between the ostensive learning of a name or mass term like 'Mama' or 'red' or 'water' and the ostensive learning of a general term like 'dog' is that the latter must go with the grain. The sustained dynamic pointing that accompanies the word 'dog', or the words 'This is a dog' or a still longer pleonasm, must not jump dogs; and it may be protracted and repeated as necessary. The similarity basis of such a term is rather sophisticated: a second-order similarity, as it were, of similarities.

We had to do in §12 with language-dependent language learning: learning that depends on other locutions previously learned. The present matter is different: a similarity of similarities. Already in learning the name 'Fido' the child depended on the similarity of one presentation of Fido to another, and of one phase of a sustained presentation of Fido to another. In learning the general term 'dog' he has to appreciate a second-order similarity between the similarity basis of 'Fido' and the similarity bases determining other enduring dogs. These various canine similarity complexes are more similar to one another, in the successful child's eye, than to the various further similarity complexes that determine the various rabbits, the various apples, the various buckles; and thus it is that the child is to master each of these general terms in the fullness of time, and to keep them properly clear of one another.

Thanks to his instinctive body-mindedness, he is an apt pupil when the general terms are terms for bodies. He is able to appreciate not only that the second-order similarity of a dog to a dog exceeds that of a dog to a rabbit, but also that the latter in turn exceeds that of a dog to an apple or buckle. Thus it is that he can learn not only the general terms 'dog' and 'rabbit' but also the more general term 'animal', which covers the dogs and the rabbits but not the apples or buckles. And then there is the yet slighter degree of second-order similarity, residing in just those very general body-unifying considerations that preserve the identity of each dog, each rabbit, each apple, each buckle, in short each body. This would be a second-order similarity basis for the child's ostensive learning of the general term 'body' itself, or 'thing', to take the likelier word.

Cutting across the dichotomy between mass terms and general terms, there is another important dichotomy: that between absolute and relative terms. Among the relative general terms a good observational example is 'smaller than'; thus 'Fido is smaller than Jumbo'. Another example, not observational, is 'mother of'. But also, what is seldom noted, there are relative mass terms; thus 'darker than'. Whereas 'mother of' or 'smaller than' relates bounded wholes, 'darker than' can relate mere points or undemarcated neighborhoods of ostension.

Like 'water', 'sugar', and 'red', the relative term 'darker than' can be taught by simple punctual ostensions. It differs only in taking the points two by two: 'Here is darker than here'. This is why I call it a relative mass term; it stands to the absolute mass terms simply as two stands to one. On the other hand the ostensive teaching of a relative general term, such as 'smaller than', calls for a pair of sweeping ostensions, adequate to suggesting the bounds of the objects concerned: 'This is smaller than this'. More restrained gestures will suffice only if the regions concerned are already salient through other causes.

'Dark' passes for an absolute mass term, and 'small' for an absolute general term, but both of them make strict sense only as relative: 'darker than', 'smaller than'. On this score they are typical of many terms. Much the same can be said even of 'red' and other color terms; red is a matter of degree. In 'redder than' we have a relative mass term, on a par with 'darker than'.

Some relative mass terms are intimately related to the individuation of absolute general terms; thus 'same dog as'. We point twice and say 'Here is the same dog as here'. I noted this idiom on an earlier page as a mere temporizing device to prolong an ostension; but we see now that it qualifies also as a relative mass observation term in its own right. This reduction of an absolute term 'dog' to a relative term 'same dog as' is an idea that I owe to Geach,[1] except that he does not distinguish between relative mass and relative general terms.

The relative mass terms 'darker than' and 'redder than' are transitive and asymmetrical. The relative mass term 'same dog as', on the other hand, is transitive and symmetrical; in a word, *equivalential*. It is these equivalential ones, as Geach observes, that provide individuation for absolute general terms.

1. "Ontological relativity and relative identity."

There is a strict formal limitation to the sort of term that can be individuated in this way. The approach fails if the term is to denote things that overlap. For consider why the relative mass term 'same dog as' suffices to individuate the dogs: each dog consists of just the points that are on the same dog as some one point. This happy circumstance depends on the fact that no dogs have points in common. A relative mass term 'same circle as' would not suffice to individuate circles, in the sense say of visibly outlined circular regions. Some of these circles may overlap, or lie one within another; and then it will not be true that each circle consists of all and only the points that are in the same circle as some one point. This characterization would miss an embedded circle altogether, and it would wrongly accord the title of circle to an oblate region built up of two overlapping circles.

The term 'circle' in the intended sense can indeed be taught by ostension, but what is wanted is a series of sweeping ostensions, each of which traces the outline and sweeps out the interior of one of the circular regions. Pairwise ostension of points is not to the purpose here, nor is a relative mass term 'same circle as'.

Absolute general terms of the type of 'dog' and 'apple', which can be taught by pairwise ostension of points, constitute an important subclass. They are probably the ones that are learned first. We gain an important insight into those terms, and into the inception of the identity concept itself, by looking to the underlying relative mass term. But afterward we must recognize the advent of further absolute general terms whose individuation calls for gestures more extravagant than pairwise pointing. Note also that the schematism of an underlying relative mass term admits of no evident extension that would implement the learning of general terms of a relative kind, such as 'smaller than'. In that example sweeping ostension was of the essence.

We have seemed to discern the inception of the identity predicate. It is a mere shared fragment of various relative mass observation terms, e.g. 'same dog as'; or, merer still, it is a temporizing vocable for prolonging an ostension. Such is the humble beginning of a predicate whose sense or utility has been pondered by Aristotle, Leibniz, Locke, Hume, Frege, Wittgenstein, and

Geach. For Locke and Hume identity made no sense except as applied to earlier and later presentations of the same body. Our present reflections on the primitive role of identity, in the individuation of bodies, fit quite well with that view. But this role is one that identity later outgrows.

Years earlier Geach argued that identity makes sense only relative to one or another general term, as in 'same dog'.[2] We have been seeing that this is decidedly true of the identity idiom at its inception. It remains true, moreover, as long as the sides of the identity sentence are demonstrative pronouns. There is no sense in pointing twice and saying 'This is the same (one) as that'; we can only ask 'Same what?' One may have pointed at the same dog and a different ear. When on the other hand we reach the sophisticated stage of making statements of identity with names on either side, or descriptions, or variables, then evidently we can affirm identities without relativizing them. We can say outright that *a* is identical with *b*; whether *a* is the same dog as *b*, or the same ear as *b*, will depend on whether *a* is a dog or an ear. When the identity idiom comes of age, Geach's old relativism evidently goes untenable. Yet there is a subtle sense in which identity is relative still. I shall take it up in §30.

§16. *Observational compounds*

Generations of linguists have rightly stressed that the distinctive trait of language, not shared by the signal systems of lower animals, is its productivity of combinations. We learn modes of composition as well as words, and are thus prepared to produce and to respond to complex expressions never heard before. One such mode of composition is what grammarians call *attributive composition*, as in 'yellow paper'. We can imagine learning it as follows. The components 'yellow' and 'paper' have separately been learned in the by now familiar way. Hearing these words enlivens traces of episodes in which yellow was salient, and episodes in which paper was salient; and these traces enhance

2. *Reference and Generality*, pp. 39f.

the salience of any yellow or paper in the present scene. Salience of yellow paper is thus enhanced doubly. All our mentor has to do to perfect our training in the compound 'yellow paper' is discourage assent in those less striking cases where the yellow and the paper are separate.

We noted (§7) that there could be heuristic value in thinking of enlivened traces as mental images. Attributive composition affords another good case. The words 'yellow' and 'paper' induce the two images, and heard together they induce them superimposed.

Other attributive compounds may be acquired individually in parallel fashion: 'red wine', 'red ball', 'white rabbit', 'sore thumb'. But the child needs to learn something more general: the art of making new attributive compounds on his own and properly responding to new ones. In learning this, as in learning assent and dissent (§12), he must be guided by a language-dependent brand of similarity. The occasions for assenting to attributive compounds are similar to one another in that they share the following complex trait: always the two component terms heighten the salience of some one part of the present scene. This account not only depends on our present reasonable doctrine that a learned word has power to enhance the salience of an appropriate part of a current episode; it also assumes that the overlapping of two such verbal heightenings would itself be noticed and used as a point of similarity.

Attributive compounds like 'yellow paper', formed of observation terms, are clearly observation terms in turn. We could learn 'yellow paper' as a whole by induction from ostensions in the familiar way, as if it were a single word. Attributive composition is just a device for the instant production of observation terms.

Observation terms may, as remarked, be viewed as observation sentences, which are a species of occasion sentences (cf. §10). 'Red', 'Mama', and the rest, seen as sentences, may also be phrased pleonastically in the manner 'Here is red', 'Red is here', 'Here is Mama'. Similarly for the compound observation term 'yellow paper': it does the work of the occasion sentence 'Here is yellow paper', 'This is yellow paper', indeed even 'This paper is yellow', 'The paper is yellow'. When rephrased in such ways, the little device of attributive composition gives our language rather a discursive air. Hitherto there had been only the abrupt style of a footman or a bird watcher, announcing or confirming arrivals. There is something less ostentatiously ostensive in the phrasing 'The paper is yellow'. Indeed no ostension is likely to be needed for the occasion sentence 'yellow paper', however phrased; for the words themselves, already familiar, heighten the salience of the yellow paper sufficiently without further help from a pointing finger. The sentence 'The paper is yellow' remains an observation sentence and occasion sentence for all that, when used as here intended. But it has the explicit form of a predication too.

In the terminology of grammar, 'yellow' is said to occur attributively in 'yellow paper' and predicatively in 'The paper is yellow'. But it seems that this distinction, like the distinction between observation term and observation sentence, has little bearing on the fundamentals of language learning.

Attributive composition affords access to a rich vein of predications. Thus take 'Mama is smiling'. 'Smiling' is an observation term that can be learned on a par with 'red', 'water', 'Mama'. We learn to apply or assent to the term when something is saliently smiling. Then 'Mama is smiling', or 'smiling Mama', comes through by attributive composition on a par with 'yellow paper', thanks to the intersecting of the pertinent saliences; the smiling occurs on Mama.

Attributive composition is one of many dyadic constructions on terms. Another is 'in'. Thus suppose we have learned 'the garden', at first not as a compound but simply as an individual name for our own garden, learned on a par with 'red' and 'Mama'. Then we learn to affirm or assent to 'Mama in the garden', or 'Mama is in the garden', just when the respective regions that are rendered salient by these two terms are combined in a certain pattern: the one surrounded by, or embedded in, the other. We generalize from various examples ⌜α in β⌝ and end up by associating 'in' with this manner of embedment.[1] The learning of

1. My convention of Greek letters and quasi quotation is explained in *Mathematical Logic*, §6. But perhaps it is already clear enough from the context.

⌜α in β⌝ is thus just like the learning of attributive composition, ⌜$\alpha\beta$⌝, except that there it was a matter merely of a partial coincidence or overlapping of the two relevant masses, while now it is a matter more specifically of an embedding of the first in the second.

Here again, and I suppose in all learning of modes of composition of expressions, we use a language-dependent kind of similarity. The occasions for the 'in' compound resemble one another by virtue only of all having this complex trait: terms are uttered whose associated portions of the scene are embedded the one in the other.

One mode of composition deserves notice because of its peculiar immediacy. It turns one observation term into another by adding the suffix '-like'. Having learned 'dog-like', 'tree-like', and a few other such cases as simple observation terms, we learn to form further such terms on our own; and the language-dependent similarity this time is curiously simple. What the proper occasions for assenting to ⌜α-like⌝ have in common is a perceptible but insufficient impulse to assent to α itself.

We are still dealing in observation terms and occasion sentences. We can still view them indifferently as terms or as sentences, unless they occur embedded in longer terms or sentences. There is no need to distinguish between the observation term 'Mama in the garden' and the occasion sentence 'Mama is in the garden', nor between 'yellow paper' and 'Yellow paper is here' or 'The paper is yellow', as long as the expression in question is not part of a longer one. But we do best not to equate the term 'yellow' or 'paper' to the sentence 'Yellow is here' or 'Paper is here' when the term stands in the broader context 'yellow paper'. While still equating the term 'yellow paper' to 'Yellow paper is here', we cannot naturally regard this sentence as a compound of 'Yellow is here' and 'Paper is here'. Certainly it is not a truth function of them. Yellow and paper may both be present, in a sweepingly ostended region, and yellow paper still be absent.

§17. *Predication and the categorical*

Observation sentences are occasion sentences, as opposed to *standing* sentences. Assent to an occasion sentence has to be prompted anew, whenever the sentence is queried, by what is currently observable. The sentence simply has no truth value apart from the occasion. A standing sentence, once assented to, remains as a standing commitment for a while at least. Among the standing sentences there are, at the extreme, the *eternal* sentences. Their truth values are fixed for good, regardless of speaker and occasion—though speakers may still disagree about them, through error, or change their minds.

An eternal sentence may be general in import, or it may report a specific local event. In the latter case it will gain its specificity through explicit use of names, dates, or addresses. The eternal sentences most characteristic of scientific theory are of course general.

Now what does language learning amount to in the case of eternal sentences? In the case of occasion sentences it amounts to learning what occasions warrant assent to the sentences, or dissent. But this opportunity for a relevant continuing check against current episodes of sensory impingements lapses when we turn to eternal sentences. We are disposed to assent to 'Dogs are animals' or 'Water is liquid' whenever asked, and this disposition leaves us no scope for semantic distinctions on the score of occasions. Eternal sentences shed the passing occasions. And simply being disposed to assent to an eternal sentence once and for all, or to dissent once and for all, surely cannot be regarded as summing up our semantic understanding of such sentences.

Assent and dissent, assertion and denial, do not exhaust the uses of sentences, not even of declarative sentences. Even an occasion sentence affirmed on a present occasion will be affirmed for an ulterior motive: perhaps for the expectation that it may engender of some future event, through systematic connections that are embodied in some rude or refined body of theory. Eternal sentences often play useful parts without being asserted or denied, believed or disbelieved, at any point. They may do their work as intermediate links in a theoretical development, e.g. as case headings: as alternative hypotheses in some dilemmatic argument by cases. Eternal sentences owe their utility to their systematic participation in theory, rude or refined, and occasion sentences owe much of *their* utility to the same. But what makes the occasion sentences less puzzling semantically than the eternal sentences is that we do not need to trace their systematic connections with theory in order to probe their meaning; they are at the periphery, where their meaning can be empirically assessed by checking them for assent and dissent, occasion by occasion. It is through this periphery that science and language imbibe all empirical content or meaning. To trace out the meaning of an eternal sentence deep inside the theory, on the other hand, we have nothing to go on but its multifarious connections within the theory and ultimately, indirectly, with the periphery. Each of these strands being describable only by its interrelations with others, there ceases to be any clear sense in asking the meaning of a single such sentence at all. The sentence can be paraphrased in terms of others of its kind, and perhaps a substantial fabric of such sentences can be given some joint explanation in terms of their combined net bearing on observations and occasion sentences.

This predicament of the semantics of eternal sentences is one that we have largely and long failed to appreciate, because of an uncritical retreat into mentalism. If ways are to be found of coping with it and developing a scientific semantics, the most hopeful approach would seem to be through a retracing, real or hypothetical, of the process by which we acquire our command of such language in the first place.

Consider, then, an example: 'Snow is white'. At the end of §7 we noted that when a word has been learned and then is heard again, it enlivens the trace of the learning episode. Intuitively speaking, the word 'snow' induces a snow image. This way of putting the matter is good, I urged, in its suggestion that the enlivened trace can have effects somewhat like those of ocular stimulation. Now such an assumption of likeness of effect stands us in good stead in explaining the learning of 'Snow is white'. The child has previously learned the observation terms 'snow' and 'white'; that is, he has learned on what occasions to assent to the query 'Snow?' and to the query 'White?'. Now the parent queries the eternal sentence 'Snow is white'. Its first word induces the snow image, and then the queried sequel 'white?' elicits the child's assent as if he were seeing snow and not just having the image.

The mechanism that I am suggesting is, in the familiar terminology, a transfer of conditioning. The child has been conditioned to assent to the query 'White?' when snow is presented, and then this response becomes transferred from the snow stimulus to the associated verbal stimulus, the word 'snow'. My account is an account of such transfer in terms of traces and salience.

In learning to understand and use the observation sentences, we depended very directly on truth-value considerations; for this learning consisted simply in learning the circumstances in which to assent to or dissent from the sentences. Coming to eternal sentences, we noticed with some misgivings that this approach was no longer suitable, because of the fixity of the truth values. But we see now that the variability of truth value has withdrawn merely to a higher level of abstraction. A predication may be saddled with one truth value for all eternity; the predicational mode of composition, however, takes on varying truth values, yielding truth for some pairs of terms and falsity for others. First and last, in learning language, we are learning how to distribute truth values. I am with Davidson here; we are learning truth conditions. In learning an occasion sentence, we learn in what circumstances to count it true and in what circumstances false. In learning the eternal predicational construction, we are learning how to judge whether a given pair of terms produces a true predication, true for good, or a false one, false for good.

The predication 'Snow is white' is the simplest sort of standing sentence, joining as it does two mass terms. The next to simplest sort is illustrated perhaps by the predication 'Fido is a dog'. Here the subject, a singular term, is on a par still with the mass terms so far as our theory of learning is concerned; but the predicate now is a general term, 'dog', involving individuation. Still, 'Fido is a dog' could be learned in much the same way as 'Snow is white'. The child has learned to assent to 'A dog?' in the presence of Fido and his ilk, and then by transfer he assents to 'A dog?' on hearing 'Fido'. He thus assents to 'Fido is a dog?'.

The case is less simple than that of 'Snow is white'. That case hinged on the child's having learned to assent to 'White?' when we point at snow. Now the child has also quite properly learned to assent to 'A dog?' when we point merely at Fido's head; but whereas any of the snow counts as white, the head is not to count as a dog. To account for the learning of 'Fido is a dog' we must look back rather to the dynamic ostension, suitably extended, that sufficed to distinguish whole dogs from heads. That was the basis of the child's learning of 'dog', and of 'Fido'. The sensed or surmised presence of Fido in all his wholeness, then, or of Fido's ilk, is what suffices to prompt assent to the query 'A dog?'. Finally, by transfer as before, the child assents to 'A dog?' on hearing the word 'Fido'. The word has induced an image of the integral animal.

Relative general terms, like absolute ones, adjoin singular terms in predication to form standing sentences; thus 'Fido is smaller than Jumbo'. Having learned the three component terms ostensively, the child could learn this standing sentence in much the same way as 'Fido is a dog'.

The next more complicated sort of predication is illustrated perhaps by 'A dog is an animal'—really a universal categorical, ⌜Every α is a β⌝. Here the subject as well as the predicate is a general term. Still, much the same learning pattern suggests itself here as in the preceding cases. Having learned the term 'animal', the child is disposed to assent to the query 'An animal?' if he surmises the presence of dogs or other animals. Then, by transfer, he comes to assent to 'An animal?' on hearing the words 'A dog'. He assents to 'A dog is an animal?'.

The child not only learns specific eternal sentences 'A dog is an animal', 'Snow is white', 'Fido is a dog', but also, by generalizing from them, he learns the modes of composition that they illustrate; for he will make further such compounds on his own. He comes to sense similarity among the ways of coming to appreciate that a dog is an animal, that snow is white, and that Fido is a dog. What he senses, as common to each such pair of terms, is perhaps a tendency in the sound of the first term to dispose him to assent to the second. Again I tread dangerous ground in speculating on inward sense. And again I plead in extenuation that it is only a question of awareness of incipient drives toward specific overt behavior.[1]

Such singular sentences as 'Fido is a dog' and 'Snow is white' must be distinguished, as eternal, from other singular sentences such as 'Fido is wet' which are occasion sentences. The sentence 'Fido is wet' resembles the standing predication 'Fido is a dog' grammatically, but psychologically it belongs rather with the attributive compounds such as 'red ball' and 'white rabbit' and, for that matter, 'Mama is in the garden'. We learn 'Fido' and 'wet' by direct exposure on a par with 'white' and 'rabbit', and then by what I described as a convergence of images we learn when to assent to 'wet Fido', or 'Fido is wet'. It is remarkable what a semantic gulf is bridged by the simple form of predication 'Fido is a dog', 'Fido is wet'. The Spaniards, with their two copulas 'es' and 'está', are more sensitive to it than we.

'Snow is white' contrasts sharply with 'The snow is white', for the latter is an observation sentence like 'The paper is yellow', a mere variant of the attributive compound 'white snow'. We should picture the child as somehow learning these predicative variants of attributive composition only well after 'Snow is white' and other eternal predications; otherwise the proposed way of learning the eternal ones would surely fail.[2]

§18. *Serendipity*

We have welcomed the idea that the sound of a word can have somewhat the same effect as the sight of its object. This has enabled us to account for the learning of standing predications and of universal categoricals. It has enabled us to bridge the gulf

1. Piaget (Chaps. 4, 7) has investigated the child's mastery of class inclusion by setting him to sorting objects. There should be a significant relation between this turning point and the mastery of the universal categorical idiom.

2. I am indebted here to Lawrence Powers.

between occasion sentences and standing sentences, putting us well on our way from observation sentence to scientific theory.

But there is a sordid side. What we have here is of the essence of the notorious confusion of sign and object, or of use and mention. Evidently this confusion, with all its evils, is integral to the very woof and (yea) warp of the fabric of science.

Language is rooted in what a good scientific language eschews. There is not just the confusion of use and mention; there is the whole matter of indicator words. Our first words as I represented them were observation terms or occasion sentences, and these are of the essence of indicator language; the occasion sentence 'red' says 'Here now red'. There is no such thing as a standing sentence until we make our faltering way to 'A dog is an animal' and 'Snow is white' and 'Fido is a dog', and this we manage only by dint of that hanky-panky over use and mention. Language is conceived in sin and science is its redemption.

Evolution by natural selection is a history of the survival of happy accidents. Man's ascent to language and to science is in kind. Truth can issue from fallacious proof. To judge the outcome by its fallacious origins is to add the genetic fallacy to what had gone before. Let us rather count our blessings.

Proverbially, what distinguishes language from its subhuman antecedents is its productivity of new combinations. But there is another distinguishing feature that is nearly as fundamental, and it is the standing sentence. The signal systems of animals are limited to simple *occasion* sentences; and such also are the human sentences on which a dog learns to act.

Serving as it does as the medium of science and history, the standing sentence—indeed the eternal sentence—must be accounted useful. It confers one conspicuous benefit straightaway in the domain of its origin, moreover, as an aid to ostension itself. Universal categoricals and standing predications serve admirably in speeding up the ostensive learning of new terms. Our teacher ostensively introduces Jumbo, gesturing and saying '[This is] Jumbo', and then, instead of persisting in dynamic gestures to point the way to the intended diachronic extrapolations, he finishes the lesson in short order by saying 'Jumbo is an animal'. Thanks to our prior acquisition of the term 'animal' with its built-in style of identifying individual animals through time, and thanks to our general acquisition of the 'is' of standing predication, we can manage all the extrapolation of 'Jumbo' ourselves on the basis of the initial ostension together with the guiding admonition 'Jumbo is an animal'.

Sometimes this expedient saves us nothing. We might successfully introduce Jumbo by a single ostension anyway, saying just 'Jumbo'—thanks to his salience and his vivid animality. But the expedient can help when a nicely salient presentation is hard to arrange.

The pair of sentences 'This is Jumbo' and 'Jumbo is an animal' admits of a familiar apocopation: 'This animal is Jumbo'.

The device helps not only when the object to be named is short on salience, but when it and other salient objects compete. Thus, to use an example I have used elsewhere, an ostension accompanied by the words 'This is Nadejda' could be misinterpreted as defining the color or the material of the woman's garment, pending further ostensions; whereas the words 'This woman is Nadejda' enable a single ostension to suffice.

The device is equally helpful in introducing new general terms. When we point to the inconspicuous form in the tree and say 'This is a marmoset', we have just begun; more lessons may be called for. But the added words 'A marmoset is an animal' would expedite matters; or, apocopating, 'This animal is a marmoset'. Some further ostension may, however, still be wanted to settle the allowable range of variation from one marmoset to another; a general term such as 'marmoset' differs from a singular term such as 'Jumbo' in having this additional degree of freedom.

In these moves one exploits the individuative force of some more general term, already learned, to obviate the separate teaching of an individuative principle for the subsumed term that one is concerned to introduce. The term 'body', because of its extreme generality, can be especially useful in this connection. We may point once and say 'This body is a buckle', or 'This body is an apple', or even 'This body is an animal'. This single ostension is likely to have settled the new term 'buckle' or 'apple' or 'animal' once and for all.

The single ostension will in some cases demand care, however, and a certain elaborateness. If one were to point to Jumbo and say 'This body is an animal', one would risk the mistake of calling Jumbo's trunk an animal; for his trunk is indeed a body in its own right, and one may in pointing out Jumbo have pointed to his trunk. But this misadventure can be avoided by a sweeping gesture. What is wanted in gestural support of the words 'This body is an animal' is ostension that is sufficiently sweeping to enhance the salience of the elephant as a whole and not just that of his trunk.

It might seem that people could have maximized this access of efficiency by learning 'body' as the first general term and then letting all the more special terms for bodies accrete parasitically: 'This body is Mama', 'This body is Fido', 'This body is an animal', 'This body is a buckle', and so on. However, there is at least one good reason why this has not happened: it presupposes a general mastery of the 'is' of standing predication. Such mastery can be acquired, it would seem, only by abstraction from a stock of separately learned examples such as 'Mama is an animal', 'Mama is a body', 'An animal is a body', 'An apple is a body', 'An elephant is an animal'. Thus, while we may exploit the term 'body' or indeed 'animal' to expedite the acquisition of further terms such as 'marmoset', 'Jumbo', 'Nadejda', it was necessary first to have acquired a representative stock of such terms the hard way.

§19. *Color and shape*

The general terms that we have been studying up to now are terms for bodies. Such terms are at the heart of individuation, given man's body-mindedness. Other general terms may have developed by analogy. But others there are. One is 'color'. Let us examine it.

'Red' was learned like 'Mama'. The two terms differed only in the course of their ostensions, as when Mama went one way and her shawl another. Moreover, just as Mama is an animal, so red is a color. But as soon as we try to treat the learning of the term 'color' in parallel to the learning of the term 'animal', curious differences emerge. In learning 'animal' we had to learn two things: (a) when an animal was being indicated at all, and (b) when the same animal was being indicated. In learning 'color' there is no parallel to (a), since color is everywhere. What then of (b), what of sameness of color? There is an odd twist of usage here. We speak of sameness of color to mean matching, and most red surfaces do not match. Sameness of color, ordinarily so called, is not sameness of color in the sense in which red is a color.

The very notion of *a* color, in the latter sense, is unnatural. Whether some arbitrary interval in the spectrum is a color, in this sense, depends on the casual matter of there being a word for it; and this matter of vocabulary varies from culture to culture. The notion of a color, in this sense, is less basic than the notion of a color word.

The color words themselves, 'red' and 'blue' and the like, are good observation terms on a par with 'water', 'Mama', 'dog', and the rest. I am not downgrading them, but rather the general term 'color' as thus applied. For an analogy, consider the people whose telephone numbers are prime. This is an unnatural notion, but the people that fall under it are real people. Correspondingly for red and blue.

Unlike the unnatural notion based on telephone numbers, the unnatural notion of color or of color word is important and useful. Like other general terms, 'color' in this sense is useful in expediting ostension. Thus take the observation sentence 'This is mauve'. It can be taught laboriously by brute ostension, repeated sufficiently to eliminate the misconception that the similarity basis might involve shape or substance or texture. By adding the eternal sentence 'Mauve is a color', the teaching is expedited.

The observation sentence and the eternal sentence apocopate in the usual way, to 'This color is mauve'. Mauve is a color in the sense in which red is a color: not a precise tint, but a vague range. Consequently the pupil may still need several exposures to get a feeling for the allowable latitude. Still, calling it a color is a big help.

Another principal use of the word 'color' is in describing something by resemblance to something familiar, as by saying that it is like an orange in color, or a pomegranate. This is not quite a matter of matching, but neither is it subject to the accidents of color words. It is a matter of chromatic similarity. Perhaps something qualifies as pomegranate-colored if it is chromatically bracketed by some pair of pomegranates; that is, if it is chromatically more similar to each of the pair than they are to each other. Chromatic similarity is fundamental to color talk, and matching is its limit. Matching is a question of "exact color" or *tint*, which is independent of vocabulary.

The word 'color' serves poorly as an observation sentence, 'Color here', 'This is a color', since, as remarked, there is color everywhere. But there are three contexts in which the word is needed and needs to be learned: '-colored' (as in 'pomegranate-colored'), 'is a color' (as in 'Red is a color'), and 'This is the same color [=tint] as this'.

Take '-colored'. First the child learns some examples as wholes in the usual ostensive way: 'orange-colored', 'coffee-colored', on a par with 'red'. Also he learns the component observation terms in the usual ostensive way: 'orange', 'coffee'. Finally he abstracts, from such examples, the art of fabricating new color terms of the form ⌜α-colored⌝ along similar lines on his own. The similarity relation that links such formations is, as at the end of §15, a similarity of similarities. The occasions for assenting to ⌜α-colored⌝ are similar to the occasions for assenting to α, and similar in a special way: chromatically. I assume, plausibly enough, that chromatic similarities bear a second-order similarity to one another. Chromatic similarities constitute, for the child, a discriminable species of similarities.

What now of the eternal sentences of the form ⌜α is a color⌝? Grammatically they are predications like 'Fido is a dog' and 'Snow is white'. These latter were handled in §17 by treating each utterance of such a sentence as an occasion sentence in which the sound of the first word is the occasion for affirming or assenting to the rest. Similarly we may treat each utterance of ⌜α is a color⌝ as an occasion sentence in which the sound of α is the occasion for affirming or assenting to 'is a color'. To master this idiom, then, the child must learn to distinguish color words from others; just that. Now the bond of similarity among the color words is their capacity to induce purely chromatic images. 'Red', for instance, enlivens the traces of episodes in which the red came in all shapes; and these shapes cancel out. Having already assumed that the child can distinguish chromatic similarity from other similarity, I do not hesitate to assume that he can distinguish chromatic images from others.

The remaining context that was to be learned is a straight observation sentence: 'This is the same color [= tint] as this'. Each occasion when this observation sentence may appropriately be assented to is an occasion of double ostension whose salient regions are chromatically similar in the extreme. So the similarity basis of this observation sentence is the second-order similarity that obtains among extreme chromatic similarities.

Along with the locutions ⌜α-colored⌝, ⌜α is a color⌝, and 'This is the same tint as this', one might look also for ⌜α is a tint⌝. Actually no use is made of this construction, outside of technical circles; names are given not to exact tints but only in a haphazard way to broader colors.

This is a point of contrast between our color vocabulary and our shape vocabulary. Terms for exact shapes are abundant: 'square', 'circle', 'parabola', 'equilateral triangle', 'Star of David', 'regular enneagon', 'sphere', 'cube', 'regular icosahedron'. This is because various specific shapes have distinctive properties of a conspicuous or useful kind, while specific tints do not, except in technical pursuits such as spectroscopy. Terms for broad ranges of shapes, analogous to the color words, are abundant too: 'oblong', 'rectangle', 'ellipse', 'triangle', 'enneagon', 'parallelepiped', 'cone', 'pyramid'.

Two useful contexts of the word 'shape' are exactly parallel in form and meaning to two of the contexts of the word 'color' that we have examined. One of them is ⌜α-shaped⌝, e.g. 'egg-shaped'. Something is perhaps egg-shaped when it is *morphically* more similar to each of some pair of eggs than they are to each other. Morphic similarities, like chromatic similarities, may be assumed to constitute for the child a discriminable species of similarities; and on that basis the child can master the idiom ⌜α-shaped⌝ in just the way that we have imagined him to master the idiom ⌜α-colored⌝.

The other useful context of 'shape' that parallels a context of 'color' is the observation sentence 'This is the same shape as this'.

The ostension accompanying this sentence would consist in the tracing of two outlines—or simply in pointing at two figures if they are already salient. The similarity basis of this observation sentence is the second-order similarity that obtains among extreme morphic similarities. Extreme morphic similarity is what geometers simply call similarity.

The idiom ⌜α is a shape⌝ is unlike ⌜α is a color⌝ because of an accident of usage. Color words, we saw, normally cover broad ranges of tints; and so it is with the α of ⌜α is a color⌝. Shape words, on the other hand, exist both for exact shapes and for ranges of shapes, and normally the context ⌜α is a shape⌝ calls for the name of an exact shape. It is natural to say 'Square is a shape'; less natural to say 'Ellipse is a shape' or 'Oblong is a shape'. The usage of 'is a shape' thus harmonizes with that of 'same shape', whereas the usage of 'is a color' was at variance with that of 'same color'.

We noted the utility of 'Mauve is a color' in expediting ostension. An idiom to similar effect is wanted in expediting ostension in the case of shape words, even when, like 'oblong', the word does not name a unique shape. 'Oblong is a shape' will not do, we saw. But something else will: we can say, outright, ' 'Oblong' is a shape word'. We already saw reason to think of ' 'Red' is a color word' as more to the point than 'Red is a color', and we can approve this resort on the same score. As for the method of learning, we have already speculated on how the child would learn ⌜α is a color⌝; it was a matter of his learning to distinguish color words from others. These speculations carry over in exact parallel to the learning of ⌜α is a shape word⌝.

There remains, then, the idiom ⌜α is a shape⌝ in its proper sense, for exact shapes: 'Square is a shape'. The child learns 'square' as an observation term, and its similarity basis is of course sameness of shape. We also had him learning the observation term 'same shape' itself; that is, the observation sentence 'This is the same shape as this'. Now in any episode of double ostension where the child is disposed to assent to 'This is the same shape as this' he is also disposed to assent to 'square' doubly or not at all. This general disposition to dispositions would be, if he could sense it, his ground for assenting to 'Square is a shape'. But it is a good deal to ask. He could learn to assent to specific cases by parroting his teacher, but he must master the principle if he is to cope with new sentences ⌜α is a shape⌝ on the strength of knowing α. Probably this is beyond him, pending mastery of other apparatus. But he already has the benefits of accelerated ostension that are afforded by the easier idiom ⌜α is a shape word⌝.

§20. *Truth functions*

We have seen nothing as yet of compound sentences, that is, sentences with other sentences as parts. 'Yellow paper', though qualifying as an occasion sentence, was seen (§16) not to contain 'yellow' and 'paper' as sentences. The simplest construction that produces sentences from sentences is *negation*. It presents a strangely simple case of learning language in relation to prior language. An occasion sentence is uttered by the pupil, or as a query by the teacher, in the presence of relevant other impingements, and the teacher or pupil dissents, saying 'no'. Already we have here a passable negation, if we just think of the occasion sentence and the dissent as joined up continuously. For it is precisely this combination that is appropriate to occasions to which the occasion sentence by itself is not. Thus we may think of our negation sign as basically a postpositive 'no'.

We have been thinking here of negation as applied to occasion sentences. It is in this application that the theory is so pat. We want the negation of an occasion sentence to be conditioned to just the occasions where the original sentence deserves a dissenting response; so the 'no' of dissent just fills the bill, here, of a postpositive negation sign. When we move out to standing sentences, this talk of occasions loses its point. Still, assent and dissent carry over to standing sentences, and with much the same force that they had for occasion sentences. When the child uttered an occasion sentence on the wrong occasion, the parent's 'no' betokened negative conditioning; it was the harbinger or accompaniment of the slap, or the substitute for it. The parent's 'no' served the same purpose when the child transgressed in other, nonsentential ways; and its force is not lost on standing sentences. On these quite as well as occasion sentences, then, the 'no' of dissent already serves automatically as a postpositive negation sign.

What of conjunction? A governing circumstance that goes far toward fixing its meaning is that a conjunction commands assent when and only when each component does. The learning is trivial; each component simply gets prompted on its own in the circumstances, and the circumstances are joint. The 'and' is pleonastic. The mechanism here is just what we saw in attributive composition or predication, 'yellow paper', 'The paper is yellow', except that there is no longer the censorship of cases where the yellow and paper are discrete. Conjunction gives 'yellow and paper', 'Here are yellow and paper', where attributive composition gave 'yellow paper', 'Here is yellow paper'. In a way the 'and' is not pleonastic after all, since it preserves this distinction. But a more natural course would have been to use an additional symbol to distinguish attributive composition, since that was where the additional consideration came in. To affirm a conjunction is simply to affirm its components, and could have been left at that if attributive composition had not intruded and pre-empted the notation of simple juxtaposition.

If we were content always to affirm conjunctions or leave them alone, then what has just been said would be the whole story. The components get affirmed, first one and then the other, and there is no cause to call this history of affirmations a compound. It is in dissent that the rub comes: if we are to dissent from a conjunction, and not just from one or other or each of its components on its own, then we need the compound to dissent from. The circumstances of dissent from a conjunction have to be mastered independently of the excessively simple rule of assent. Still, one of the rules of dissent is simple enough: the conjunction commands dissent whenever a component does. This is a uniformity which, though language-dependent, would be quickly learned: people, whenever queried, are observed to dissent from a conjunction in all circumstances where they dissent from either component.

Conjunction has its blind spot, however, where neither component commands assent nor dissent. There is no direct way of mastering this quarter. In some such cases the conjunction commands dissent and in others it commands nothing. This sector is mastered only later in theory-laden ways. Where the components are 'It is a mouse' and 'It is a chipmunk', and neither is affirmed nor denied, the conjunction will still be denied. But where the components are 'It is a mouse' and 'It is in the kitchen', and neither is affirmed nor denied, the conjunction will perhaps be left in abeyance.

A contrast thus emerges between truth functions and something more primitive, *verdict functions*. Verdict logic is three-valued, the three verdicts being assent, dissent, and abstention. A compound sentence is a verdict function of its components if a verdict to the compound is determined for each assignment of verdicts to the components. Negation is at once a verdict function and a truth function. The verdict to the compound is assent, abstention, or dissent according as the verdict to the component is dissent, abstention, or assent. Conjunction, on the other hand, is a truth function that does not quite qualify as a verdict function. Its verdict table is incomplete, as follows.

p \ *q*	assent	abstain	dissent
assent	assent	abstain	dissent
abstain	abstain	?	dissent
dissent	dissent	dissent	dissent

What now of alternation? The question how we learn alternation is of little moment, since we *could* construct it from negation and conjunction in the well-known way. Let us then just pause to observe that its behavior under assent and dissent is similar and dual to that of conjunction. Alternation, like conjunction, has its blind quarter where neither component commands assent nor dissent. We might assent to the alternation of 'It is a mouse' and 'It is a chipmunk', or we might abstain. The incomplete verdict table for alternation is as follows.

p \ *q*	assent	abstain	dissent
assent	assent	assent	assent
abstain	assent	?	abstain
dissent	assent	abstain	dissent

Verdict functions approximating to conjunction and alternation could be forged by specifying abstention at the center of the tables. These are more primitive than the genuine truth-functional conjunction and alternation, in that they can be learned by induction from observation of verdictive behavior. They are independent of our parochial two-valued logic, and independent of other truth-value logics. Truth values represent a more advanced, more theory-laden level of linguistic development; and it is in terms of theory, different theories for different subject matters, that we eventually learn (if at all) what verdict to give to the cases of conjunction and alternation that are indeterminate at the center of the verdict tables. Two-valued logic is a theoretical development that is learned, like other theory, in indirect ways upon which we can only speculate. Some theorists, notably the intuitionists, favor another logic, and there is nothing in the observable circumstances of our utterances that need persuade them to assign meaning to our two-valued scheme.

§21. *Analyticity*

Carnap maintained, and Frege before him, that the laws of logic held by virtue purely of language: by virtue of the meanings of the logical words. In a word, they are analytic. I have protested more than once that no empirical meaning has been given to the notion of meaning, nor, consequently, to this linguistic theory of logic. But now in terms of the learning process can we perhaps find some sense for the doctrine? We learn the truth functions, I just now suggested, by finding connections of dispositions; e.g. that people are disposed to assent to an alternation when disposed to assent to a component. The law that an alternation is implied by its components is thus learned, we might say, with the word 'or' itself; and similarly for the other laws.

Some such linking of meaning and truth is of course characteristic of language learning generally, also apart from the logical particles. We learn to understand and use and create declarative sentences only by learning conditions for the truth of such sentences. This is evident enough in the earliest language learning, the learning of observation sentences, since such learning is simply a matter of learning the circumstances in which those sentences count as true. The case is not quite thus with eternal sentences, since the truth value of an eternal sentence does not vary with circumstances. Still, the learning of 'A dog is an animal' as I represented it consisted in learning to assent to it, and this hinged on the truth of the sentence. It hinged anyway on our having learned to assent to 'dog' only in circumstances in which we learned also to assent to 'animal'. If we learned to use and understand 'A dog is an animal' in the way I described, then we learned at the same time to assent to it, or account it true.

It would seem reasonable, invoking the controversial notion of analyticity, to say that by this account the sentence 'A dog is an animal' is analytic; for to learn even to understand it is to learn that it is true. Where the rub comes, however, is in numbers: the number of different universal categorical sentences and the number of persons learning them. My hypothesis is that each of us learns his first few universal categorical sentences in the described way, but that different persons will begin with different sentences. Afterward, by abstraction from such samples, each of us masters the universal categorical construction as such, and is able to form new universal categoricals on a do-it-yourself basis. This general mastery of the universal categorical construction brings mastery of countless universal categorical sentences that no one would call analytic nor even true. If the samples first acquired qualify as analytic, still they gain thereby no distinctive status with respect to the language or the community; for each of us will have derived his universal categorical powers from different first samples. Language is social, and analyticity, being truth that is grounded in language, should be social as well. Here then we may at last have a line on a concept of analyticity: a sentence is analytic if *everybody* learns that it is true by learning its words. Analyticity, like observationality, hinges on social uniformity.

The formulation wants some refining. We should limit the people to those who learn the language as mother tongue. Also we should allow for chains of proof; we would want a recondite sentence to count still as analytic if obtainable by a chain of inferences each of which individually is assured by the learning of the words.

Perhaps this version of analyticity succeeds in drawing a rough line between sentences like 'No bachelor is married' or 'We are our cousins' cousins', which are ordinarily said to be analytic, and sentences that are not. At any rate it would seem that we all learned 'bachelor' uniformly, by learning that our elders are disposed to assent to it in just the circumstances where they will assent to 'unmarried man'.

In making analyticity hinge thus on a community-wide uniformity in the learning of certain words, we reopen the question of analyticity of logical truths; for what about disagreement over logical truths, e.g. on the part of intuitionists? We should find perhaps that some logical truths are analytic and some not. I suggested in particular that we do learn that an alternation is implied by its components, with the very learning of the word 'or'; and this is all very well, for it is a logical law that the intuitionists do not contest. I suggest that the law of excluded middle, which they do contest, is not similarly bound up with the very learning of 'or' and 'not'; it lies rather in the blind quarter of alternation. Perhaps then the law of excluded middle, though true by our lights, should be seen as synthetic.

In *Word and Object* I defined a *stimulus-analytic* sentence as one to which every speaker is disposed to assent. The analytic sentences in the present sense are a subclass of those, and a somewhat nearer approximation to the analytic sentences uncritically so called. Even so, we have here no such radical cleavage between analytic and synthetic sentences as was called for by Carnap and other epistemologists. In learning our language each of us learns to count certain sentences, outright, as true; there are sentences whose truth is learned in that way by many of us, and there are sentences whose truth is learned in that way by few or none of us. The former sentences are more *nearly* analytic than the latter. The *analytic* sentences are the ones whose truth is learned in that way by all of us; and these extreme cases do not differ notably from their neighbors, nor can we always say which ones they are.

part III referring to objects

§22. *Narrowing the subject*

We have been speculating on the mechanisms of language learning, with emphasis on cognitive language. Our general objective was a better understanding of how scientific theory can have been achieved. We have now reached the end of our speculations on the primitive steps. Our speculations on the subsequent steps toward theoretical language will be limited to one important aspect: the referential aspect, the acquisition of an apparatus for speaking of objects. Somehow we do learn to speak effortlessly of objects, and not only of physical objects but of attributes, numbers, sets, all sorts of abstract objects. To what do we owe all this virtuosity of objective reference, and wherein does it consist?

When can a child be said to have learned to refer to the color red? Suppose he has learned to respond, on demand, in distinctive verbal ways according as red is conspicuously present or not.

Can we then say that he has learned to refer to red? No, this is not enough for what I mean by reference. We can credit the child at this point with being able to *discriminate* red, to *recognize* red. We in conferring these credits do refer to the child and to the color; these references we will readily own. But to say that he refers to the color would be to impute our ontology to him.

The gratuitousness of thus imputing our ontology can be appreciated by considering in place of the child a foreign adult who gives similar evidence of recognizing red. There is a verbal response that he makes on demand in case red is present and not otherwise. Must this response be construed as a name of the color? Might it not be, instead, a general term by which he denotes each red portion of surface? or a general term by which he denotes each whole visible red patch but no smaller parts of such patches? or a general term by which he denotes each body that shows a conspicuously red portion of surface? or a general term by which he denotes each whole episode or specious present that flaunts red conspicuously? Under these different choices the object of reference varies. Under the one choice it is a color. Under other choices it is a patch, and a different patch from occasion to occasion. Under still other choices it is a body, or an episode, and a different one from occasion to occasion.

Thus, while we may determine straightforwardly enough that a given word of the foreigner's language serves to attest to the presence of red, this leaves us a long way from settling what thing or things, abstract or concrete, his word may refer to, if indeed to any. We would settle this rather by working up a manual of English translation for a substantial portion of the foreigner's language. Within that systematic structure, the word that we were worrying about would be given an English translation compatible with the role that the word plays in that broader setting. Then, presumably, we could answer the question of reference.

We could come out with different answers by developing different manuals of translation, each consistent with the man's verbal behavior. Such is the doctrine of indeterminacy of translation that I have urged elsewhere; it will not be a theme of this book. What I want to bring out now is merely that the reference of the foreigner's word is not settled by his use of it in attesting to the presence of red, and that the reference is settled only by translating a good deal of the foreign linguistic apparatus.

The cases of our own small child and that of the adult foreigner are superficially alike: each of these persons has mastered a word attesting to the presence of red. But the two cases differ in that the reference of the foreigner's word has yet to be assessed, whereas the reference of the child's word has yet to be acquired. Assessment of the reference of the foreigner's word awaits only our systematic English manual of translation of his elaborate language. Such a manual would enable us to fall back upon our familiar English referential apparatus and so decide whether to regard his word as designating the color red or as denoting patches or as denoting bodies or whatever. Different manuals may lead to different answers, but one will do. The child, on the other hand, is too young to have acquired any apparatus, English or otherwise, whereby to distinguish among these various possible references. We can credit him with the knack of responding distinctively to red episodes, but there the credit stops.

I shall speculate on the steps by which the child might progress from that primitive stage until we are satisfied by his easy communication with us that he has mastered our apparatus of reference. Thus I shall be concerned only with our language, not with translation. I spoke of translation from the foreigner's language just in order to make one point clear: to show that reference involves more than the simple ability to acknowledge a presence. I showed this by pointing out that a word adequate to acknowledging red episodes could be drawn from any of various referential roles; and I needed the foreign setting so as to keep the question of reference open. Now that this point is made, I can forget about foreign languages and translation.

It may be objected that adherence to the home language affords no escape from theoretical problems of translation, since we are in principle still translating from idiolect to idiolect even if our manual of translation happens to be the null manual of homophonic translation, the identity transformation. Well, this last part is true: the indeterminacy of translation holds also at home. But adherence to the home language can nevertheless afford escape from problems of translation. It all depends on what we are trying to do. It depends on whether we are going to make capital of relations of sameness and difference of meaning. In translation we do, whereas here I shall not. I shall be speculating on the steps by which I may plausibly have got to the point of bandying certain portions of English as I do—portions that I call the referential apparatus and can roughly specify by enumerating some English pronouns, copulas, plural endings. I shall be equally interested in the steps by which you all may plausibly have arrived at much the same usage as mine; but the sameness that I have in mind here is merely the sameness that is tested by smoothness of dialogue, and not a sameness of hidden meanings.

The child learns this apparatus by somehow getting a tentative and faulty command of a couple of its component devices, through imitation or analogy perhaps, and then correcting one against the other, and both against the continuing barrage of adult precept and example, and going on in this way until he has a working system meeting social standards. This is a vague picture of how it has to be. I want a less vague picture. This referential part of language learning needs to be better understood because it is so central to our conceptual scheme. Our understanding of the psychogenesis of reference could enhance our understanding of reference itself, and of ontology: of what it means to posit something. It could enhance our understanding, in particular, of universals.

§23. *General and singular*

What is the referential apparatus? I mentioned pronouns, plural endings, copulas. There is the copula of identity and there is the copula of predication that joins general terms to singular terms. Also the contrast between general and singular term is itself part of the mechanism.

A general term is true of any number of objects, from none up. A singular term designates a single object, when all goes well. Predication joins the two terms to form a sentence to the effect that this designated object is one of the objects of which the general term is true.

'Mama' and 'Fido' are singular terms, though our categorizing them as such is a sophisticated bit of retrospection that bears little relevance to what the learning child is up to. 'Animal', 'dog', 'apple', 'buckle', and 'body' are general terms, retrospectively speaking, and what makes them so is the built-in individuation.

In these examples the objects are bodies. The general terms are true of bodies and the singular terms 'Mama' and 'Fido' designate bodies, one apiece. But those two singular terms were learned as observation sentences in the same way as other observation sentences, such as 'red' and 'water' and 'It is raining', that do not designate bodies. Recurrence of Mama or Fido was recurrence of a recognizable circumstance, like recurrence of red or rain. Thus the learning of these singular terms had nothing distinctive to do with objective reference. It is rather the learning of the first general terms, as we now call them, that may be said to bring the child a step nearer to our patterns of objective reference, because of the individuation.

Individuation is initially the one feature that distinguishes general from singular: 'dog' from 'Fido'. Their difference of role in predication is not significant at first, because the way of learning the predication 'Fido is a dog' or 'Fido is an animal' is not significantly different from the way of learning 'A dog is an animal' or 'Snow is white'.

'Snow', 'water', 'white', and 'red' can be learned in the simple manner of 'Fido' and 'Mama'. These all start out on a par, with no thought of designation and no premium on bodies. The early individuative terms, on the other hand, are general terms for bodies. Bodies are the charter members of our ontology, let the subsequent elections and expulsions proceed as they may.

'Color' seems, superficially, to be a general term on a par with the ones for bodies. 'Red' was quite like 'Fido' in manner of learning, and 'Red is a color' matches 'Fido is a dog' in form. The sameness of form is no accident; the syntactical behavior of the term 'color' follows the analogy of general terms for bodies. But we found (§19) that the term 'color' was defective: it did not admit of the context 'This is a color', whereas 'This is a dog', 'This is an apple', etc. were basic contexts for these general terms for bodies. And we found even that 'Red is a color', 'Mauve is a color', etc. were false fronts in a way; they were curiously language-bound. ' 'Red' is a color word', ' 'Mauve' is a color word' seemed more to the point.

Language thrives on analogical formation. The surface resemblance of the grammar of the term 'color' to the grammar of the general terms for bodies is quite the way of language, and it is not to be set down to some early belief that colors, like bodies, were objects. I think matters developed in the opposite order. As one came increasingly to think in referential ways, one came to objectify colors along with bodies on the strength of the superficial grammatical parallels.

'Shape' is another term that seems superficially to behave like the general terms for bodies. When we looked deeper we found it intermediate in behavior between 'color' and the body terms. It resists the context 'This is a shape'; on this score it is like 'color'. On the other hand predications such as 'Square is a shape' have none of the language-bound character of 'Red is a color'; they have rather the objectivity of 'Fido is a dog' and other predications regarding bodies.

So much for the analogy between 'Square is a shape' and 'Fido is a dog'. Observe now a conflicting analogy that casts 'square' in the role no longer of 'Fido' but of 'dog'. We can point and say 'This is a square', 'This is the same square as this', every bit as significantly as 'This is a dog', 'This is the same dog as this'. 'Square' individuates. We have to learn when we are pointing twice to the same square and when to two squares. We can say 'Hoboken is square', or 'Hoboken is a square', quite on a par with 'Fido is a dog'. In these ways 'square' is unlike 'Fido', 'red', 'snow', and 'white', and like 'dog', 'animal', and 'tint'. 'Square' is a general term after all, by our best criterion thus far: individuation.

Logicians resolve this conflict of analogies by declaring an ambiguity. 'Square' is general in 'This is a square' and in 'This is the same square as this', they declare, and singular in 'Square is a shape'. They dispel the ambiguity when they wish by rendering the singular term as 'squareness'. It is an abstract singular term, they say, in contrast to the concrete singular term 'Fido'. It is abstract by virtue of its intimate connection with a general term, 'square'. Here is that first portentous step down the primrose path of abstract ontology. Shapes are abstract objects, universals; and squareness is one of them.

'Square' and other shape words afford thus an entering wedge for Platonism. Color words would not have done so. Formally the difference is that a union of patches of a given color preserves the color, while a union of patches of a given shape does not preserve the shape. We can speak of snow as white and of blood as red without treating 'white' and 'red' as general terms. We can treat 'white' and 'red' as on a par with 'snow' and 'blood'. Snow is a scattered portion of the world that is part of a more extensive scattered portion of the world, the white. Similarly for blood and red. Similarly for Mama smiling and Mama, for that matter, except that the temporal scatter of Mama's comings and goings gets taken up into a spatiotemporal continuity as science advances. Fido's being a dog, on the other hand, does not come down to his being part of that more extended part of the world that is made up of dogs; for this could be said also of each of his ears. Similarly for something's being square.

'Dog', though individuative like 'square', would not have served Platonism as entering wedge for another reason: 'dog' is less likely than 'square' to be drawn into the role of singular term as subject of a predication. 'Dog is a species' is unlikely in early discourse; 'Square is a shape' is more likely. 'Dogs are animals' is of course beside the point; the various dogs are various animals. What 'Square is a shape' says is that square or squareness is a single shape, as Fido is a single animal.

'Dogs are numerous' is indeed a fair analogue of 'Square is a shape', for it cannot be read as qualifying each separate dog. It is on a par rather with 'Dog is a species', or 'Dogs are a species', and it has the advantage of being likely even in early discourse. If its idiomatic form had been 'Dog is numerous', like 'Square is a shape', it would have been a good wedge for Platonism too.

Once the wedge is in, analogy drives it further. Color words come to be thought of as general terms, so that 'Snow is white' and 'Blood is red' are assimilated to 'Fido is an animal' instead of being seen as mere subsumptions of one mass term under another. And then the color word in subject position, 'Red is a color', comes to count as an abstract singular term like 'square' in 'Square is a shape' rather than a concrete one as in 'Fido is an animal'.

Under ordinary usage, we see, the contrast between concrete general and abstract singular terms is indistinct. Identity, another component of our referential mechanism, likewise fogs up under ordinary usage. Often we speak seemingly of objects of one or another queer sort for which we can supply no principle of individuation. Take characters of fiction. Do two drafts of a novel have the same hero? How dissimilar can they be? For that matter, how dissimilar can the drafts be and still be drafts of the same novel? Or take gods. Was Baal the devil? Were the Algonquins, in their worship of the Great Spirit, worshipping God? All these examples belong under the general head of identity between individuals in different possible words. To turn to a soberer example, take attributes. Coextensiveness of attributes does not make them the same attribute; but then what does? We are fobbed off with the answer 'necessary coextensiveness', but this only puts another name to the problem.

Putting our house in ontological order is not a matter of making an already implicit ontology explicit by sorting and dusting up ordinary language. It is a matter of devising and imposing. Genetically what we have beforehand is just a play of grammatical analogies that mask differences in learning patterns. Centrally situated there is what we retrospectively classify as talk of bodies. Here is where the apparatus of objective reference gets its first development. Bodies are the prime reality, the objects *par excellence*. Ontology, when it comes, is a generalization of somatology. Steps in this direction have already occurred in the development of ordinary language, in the emergence of such general terms as 'color' and 'shape' by grammatical analogy to the general terms for bodies. In forging this grammatical analogy we make our first faltering allusion to incorporeal things. Grammar is thereby simplified, while ontology is multiplied.

Science seeks organization and simplicity. In this spirit the ontologist may try to render our ontology less heterogeneous. He finds a fairly natural way, perhaps, of generalizing some one of his categories so as to cause it to subsume another of his categories. Thus he generalizes body to *physical object*, taking this term broadly enough to admit as a physical object any material aggregate however scattered; and thereupon he is able to treat a mass term such as 'water' or 'sugar' as a singular term designating a single diffuse object.

It is in deliberately ontological studies that the idea of objective reference gains full force and explicitness. The idea is alien to large parts of our ordinary language. Still it has its roots in ordinary language. A distinction between concrete general and abstract singular is sometimes visible in ordinary usage, and clean-cut standards of individuation are implicit in ordinary usage for wide ranges of objects. It is in imposing this referential pattern all across the board that scientific theory departs from ordinary language. We see the result: objective reference is central to our scientific picture of the world. This is why it seems desirable to trace the roots of reference in language learning.

§24. *Relative clauses*

The pronoun was one of the items that I mentioned as making up the referential apparatus. It has a crucial place in that apparatus, as we shall see, and it is the prototype of the variable of logic and mathematics. In ordinary language it does its important work as an adjunct of the relative clause. So I propose to speculate on the learning of the relative clause.

First let us look to its function. We have a complex sentence about some object, say Fido, and the object is mentioned deep inside the sentence, or mentioned more than once; say 'I bought Fido from a man that found him'. Then the relative clause enables us to segregate the object from what the sentence says about it. We get the relative clause, 'that I bought from a man that found him', from the sentence by substituting the relative pronoun 'that' or 'which' for the name of the object (and then moving this pronoun to the front). This relative clause serves as a general term which, when predicated of the object (Fido), reaffirms the original sentence.

Geach has well argued, to the contrary, that the relative clause is not a general term.[1] He would equate the relative pronoun 'that', in 'I bought Fido from a man that found him', to 'and he'; thus 'I bought Fido from a man *and he* [had] found him. In other examples he equates 'that' (or 'which' or 'who') to 'and it', or 'if he', or 'if it', or 'since he'; but always to a conjunction (in the grammarian's sense of the word) paired with a simple pronoun. On this view, which Geach calls the *Latin prose theory* of relative pronouns, it is wrong to treat 'that found him' or 'man that found him' as a term or as a self-contained grammatical entity at all. For, to switch to a mediaeval example that he adduces, take 'man that owns a donkey'—as if to say 'donkey-owner'. The sentences:

> Any man that owns a donkey beats it,
>
> Some man that owns a donkey does not beat it

would reduce to nonsense:

> Any donkey-owner beats it,
>
> Some donkey-owner does not beat it.

On his analysis, which renders 'that' as 'if he' or 'and he' and includes changes in word order, the sentences remain coherent:

> Any man, *if he* owns a donkey, beats it.
>
> Some man owns a donkey *and he* does not beat it.

A more challenging example, adapted by Geach from Emmon Bach, runs thus:

> A boy that was only fooling her kissed a girl
> that really loved him.

We cannot treat 'boy that was only fooling her' as a term in its own right, failing a reference for the dangling pronoun 'her'; nor can we seek that reference in 'girl that really loved him', failing a reference for the dangling pronoun 'him'. This reciprocal passing of the buck is nicely resolved by Geach's analysis:

1. *Reference and Generality*, pp. 115-122; also "Quine's syntactical insights."

A boy kissed a girl *and she* really loved him
but he was only fooling her.

Geach's analysis resolves out the relative clauses and accords prior status to quantification. For the above four paraphrases along his line amount to these:

(1) $(\exists x)$ (x is a man and I bought Fido from x and x had found Fido),

(2) (x) (y) (if x is a man and y is a donkey and x owns y then x beats y),

(3) $(\exists x)$ $(\exists y)$ (x is a man and y is a donkey and x owns y and not (x beats y)),

(4) $(\exists x)$ $(\exists y)$ (x was a boy and y was a girl and x kissed y and y really loved x but x was only fooling y).

The clearest and neatest account of the grammar of a fully acquired language is one thing; the most plausible account of the child's steps of acquisition of that grammar, or of the historical stages of its evolution, is another. Harmony between the two accounts would be gratifying and reassuring. According to Halle, Chomsky, and Bloomfield, it should be sought and expected.[2] In the present instance, however, I favor a contrary position: a dualistic one. I accept Geach's Latin prose theory as a description of the accomplished grammatical fact, and I find at the same time that the steps of acquisition are most readily imagined by assimilating the primitive relative clauses to general terms. Most contexts in which we use relative clauses, and all the simplest ones, are contexts like the Fido example, which submit indifferently to the view of relative clauses as general terms and to the Latin prose theory. I picture the child as mastering this much and then being led on by evident analogies to further contexts where crucial pronouns stray irrecoverably afield, as in Geach's three examples. I picture him as being thus lured by analogies between 'that' or 'which', on the one hand, and 'and he', 'if it', etc. on the other—the very analogies that afterward become the central structure of the finished grammar of relative terms in Geach's formulation.

2. See Halle's paper and his references.

The following considerations incline me to this theory of the learning process. We cannot easily picture the child as learning the relative pronoun initially as a versatile surrogate for 'and he', 'if it', 'since he', and the rest, when we consider the complex dependence of these alternatives upon differences of context. Furthermore, if the child did manage to begin thus, he would still have to learn the quantificational idioms as of (1)-(4), or their vernacular equivalents, before learning relative clauses. The one course of plausibly short steps of transformation and analogy that I have managed to devise, leading ultimately to a command of something equivalent to quantification, is a course that achieves the relative clause first and then moves with its help to quantification.

Anyway I am not bent even upon a factual account of the learning of English, welcome though it would be. My concern with the essential psychogenesis of reference would be fulfilled in fair measure with a plausible account of how one might proceed from infancy step by step to a logically regimented language of science, even bypassing English. This terminal language could very well have complex general terms as its nearest analogues of relative clauses, without prejudice to a Latin prose theory of proper English.

§25. *Substitution and 'such that'*

Let us proceed, then, with our psychogenetic speculations. I shall not quite desert English, but with a view to the woods as over against the trees I shall depart from the most idiomatic English. Already in English there is a variant of the relative clause that obeys somewhat simpler rules: the 'such that' construction. It differs none from the idiomatic relative clause in respect of Geach's strictures, but it is simpler in word order. In this idiom the relative clause 'that I bought from a man that found him' becomes 'such that I bought him from a man that found him'. Here the word order of the original sentence about Fido is preserved: 'I bought him from a man that found him', 'I bought Fido from a man that found him'.

Tangles of cross-reference quickly arise, in the 'such that' construction no less than in ordinary relative clauses. This is illustrated already by our present example, as soon as we put the part 'that found him' into the 'such that' idiom. We get 'such that I bought him from a man such that he found him': who whom? Well, it is mainly mathematicians that talk in 'such that's, and they settle matters by turning their pronouns to bound variables: 'x such that I bought x from a man y such that y found x'. This, the 'such that' construction with bound variables, is the rectified relative clause, rid of crotchets that could only complicate our speculations on the essential psychogenesis of reference. Let us hereafter picture relative clauses thus, as if the child were growing up directly into this idiom instead of the traditional one.

The relative clause enables us to put any sentence about an object *a* into the form of a predication, '*a* is *P*', where '*P*' is a general term. It enables us to render 'I bought Fido from a man that found him' as a predication, 'Fido *is* such that I bought him from a man that found him'. Here the relative clause, or 'such that' clause, figures as a general term in adjectival form. To turn it into substantival form, which will be more useful hereafter, we merely apply an adaptor, the word 'thing': thus 'Fido is a thing such that I bought it from a man that found it'. Dog lovers will please excuse my sudden depersonalization of Fido; it will be helpful to waive logically insignificant distinctions. Anyway, the 'it' is on its way out now in favor of variables: 'Fido is a thing x such that I bought x from a man that found x'.

To say that the relative clause enables us to put any sentence about *a* into the form of a predication, '*a* is *P*', is not to say that we should want to. The utility of the relative clause lies rather in contexts where the clause is not thus predicated, but where it plays rather one of the other roles of a general term. Now one such role is that of the α of the universal categorical construction, ⌜An α is a β⌝, ⌜Every α is a β⌝. This is not a predication. It couples two general terms.

Thus take the sentence 'Everything that we salvaged from the wreck is in the shed'. If this example is to make sense as a universal categorical, ⌜Every α is β⌝, we need a general term to play the role of α; and the term for the purpose is precisely the relative clause 'thing that we salvaged from the wreck'. Regimented in our 'such-that' idiom, it is 'thing x such that we salvaged x from the wreck'. The whole sentence now runs: 'Everything x such that we salvaged x from the wreck is in the shed'. Clearly the utility of the universal categorical construction depends heavily on this use of relative clauses.

How, then, may the child have learned the relative clause? The obvious way is by an equivalence transformation. The mechanism of learning an equivalence transformation seems simple: the learner is merely brought to see, by abundant examples, the interchangeability of certain constructions. What he is brought to see for our present purposes is that we can interchange 'I see the moon' with 'The moon is a thing that I see', or, in our regimentation, 'The moon is a thing x such that I see x'. We can interchange 'Fa' with 'a is a thing x such that Fx'. It is a substitution transformation: substitution of 'a' for 'x' in 'Fx'. The child learns this transformation by finding inductively that people will, if asked, assent to 'Fa' in all and only the situations where they will assent to 'a is a thing x such that Fx'. He learns in context, in this way, the relative clause 'thing that I see' and indeed the general construction 'thing x such that Fx'. He learns it in just the predication context, this being the context in which the relative clause is explained away by the substitution transformation.

The acquisition would have little value if the child left it at that. Why say 'The moon is a thing that I see' when you can say 'I see the moon'? The substitution transformation explains the relative clause in just the one position, the predicative, where it is useless. This is no coincidence; the clause is useless there because the equivalence transformation can eliminate it there. What gives the relative clause its utility is something else: the child's pursuit of analogy. General terms and relative clauses take predicate position; so relative clauses are analogous to general terms; so the child lets the relative clause into other positions, notably in the categorical construction, where he is accustomed to using general terms. More exactly, what he does is to emulate his elders in this maneuver without excessive bewilderment, thanks to the analogy and despite there being no equivalence transformation to explain the relative clauses away from these contexts.

The substitution transformation that starts the relative clause on its way could be used more liberally if one did not care about producing something analogous to a general term. The transformation carried '*Fa*' into '*a* is a thing *x* such that *Fx*'. The words '*a* is a thing *x* such that' (or '*a* is a thing that') serve, we see, as a substitution operator; here is the essence of the relative clause. Apply the operator to '*Fx*' and you get '*Fa*'. To stress this substitutional aspect, let us temporarily condense the words '*a* is a thing *x* such that' to read simply '*a* vicè *x*'. This is the Latin *vice*, which I pronounce [vaɪ:si] *more anglico*. The result of applying this substitution operator '*a* vicè *x*' to an expression does not *designate* the result of substitution; it in effect *is* the result of the substitution. '*Fa*' is equated to '*a* vicè *x Fx*', or '*a* is a thing *x* such that *Fx*'. 'I see the moon' is equated to 'The moon vicè *x* I see *x*'. Now that the words 'thing' and 'such that' are suppressed from view, we can easily dissociate our '*a*' and '*x*' from the category of singular terms; for this substitution operator makes sense for any grammatical category. You could transform 'How do you do' and say 'Do vicè *x* how *x* you *x*'.

The relative clause was learned in predicate position but became useful by wandering from predicate position, in emulation of general terms; by wandering into the categorical. In so doing it lost its eliminability. There is no lure, similar to the general term, to unsettle this more general substitution operator '*a* vicè *x*'. Even so, it can get itself into inextricable positions. Consider this combination: '(*x x* vicè *x*) vicè *x x* vicè *x*'. Bewildering? Well, we have our instructions; let us carry out the indicated substitution and see what the result says. If you try it on paper you come out with just what you started with: '(*x x* vicè *x*) vicè *x x* vicè *x*'.[1]

Thus far, little harm. Failure of eliminability had to be faced anyway when the relative clause wandered into the categorical. But there is worse ahead, as you will guess: Russell's paradox.

1. The parentheses can be mechanized by writing this as '(*x x* vicè *x*) vicè (*x x* vicè *x*)', and '*a* vicè *x Fx*' in general as '*a* vicè (*x Fx*)'.

Just repeat my earlier example with two negation signs inserted: '(*x* not (*x* vicè *x*)) vicè *x* not (*x* vicè *x*)'. It prescribes a substitution which, when carried out, produces the negation of the whole formula itself.

Our child could learn this general substitution operator, '*a* vicè *x*', as easily as he learned the relative clause. For the words '*a* is a thing *x* such that' are just a special case of '*a* vicè *x*'; they are the case for singular terms. The equivalence transformation by which the general case would be learned is just the same, and in fact the general case '*a* vicè *x*' is easier than the special case in not being followed up by analogical extension to other than substitutional contexts.

There, then, but for the grace of God, goes our child, blithely down the garden path and into the very jaws of Russell's paradox. Or maybe he would be stopped short by a saving quality of realistic level-headedness or want of imagination. Up to a point he would take the 'vicè' construction in his stride because he can eliminate it by carrying out the substitution, but maybe his tolerance of it would lapse when the case was so farfetched that he could not see for the life of him how to eliminate it even from full substitution contexts.[2] Maybe this would happen already in the affirmative case, which was irresoluble and queer even though not yet self-contradictory. '*x x* vicè *x* indeed!' he lisps indignantly, and it warms one's heart to hear him. Or if, headlong and unheeding, he extrapolates too far, he is presently confounded by the paradox and thus receives his overdue lesson in critical thinking.

The paradox is not quite the same as Russell's, since this idiom is one of sheer substitution. There is no appeal to classes, no clear case of objective reference at all, nor any intrusion of semantic concepts. It is interesting that the paradox can be got at this level.

In any event the paradox goes ungrammatical when we confine the substitution operator to the 'such that' case, the case where the variable takes the position of singular terms. Transcribed for this case, the previously paradoxical line would run thus:

2. This criterion of meaninglessness is reminiscent of Church on lambda conversion. See his page 17.

(thing x such that x is not a thing x such that) is a thing x such that x is not a thing x such that.

One is prepared to find this ungrammatical.

The runaway substitution operator 'a vicè x' has 'a is a thing x such that' as its special case where 'a' represents a singular term and 'x' takes the positions of singular terms. This is the case that accounts for relative clauses, and it is innocent of paradox. It is so innocent that it can be translated into elementary logic as '$(\exists x)$ ($a = x$ and', or, equivalently, as '(x) (if $a = x$ then'; for

$$Fa \equiv (\exists x)\,(a = x \text{ and } Fx) \equiv (x)\,(\text{if } a = x \text{ then } Fx).$$

But this translation does not depict the learning process. Quantification is a later acquisition.

§26. *Quantifiers and variables*

In §17 we speculated on how the child might master the universal affirmative categorical construction, ⌜Every α is a β⌝. Now an application of the 'such that' construction, or relative clause, may be seen in the derivation of the other categorical forms. Where the general term β in ⌜Every α is a β⌝ is the relative clause ⌜thing x such that x is not a γ⌝, the whole becomes

⌜Every α is a thing x such that x is not a γ⌝,

which may be abbreviated as ⌜No α is a γ⌝—the universal negative categorical. The two particular categoricals, then, ⌜Some α is a γ⌝ and ⌜Some α is not a β⌝, are got by negating the sentences ⌜No α is a γ⌝ and ⌜Every α is a β⌝.

Quantification is forthcoming too. This was already evident in §25 from the example 'Everything that we salvaged from the wreck is in the shed', for it amounts to a universally quantified conditional. In general the universally quantified conditional '(x) (if Fx then Gx)' is forthcoming as a universal categorical ⌜Every α is a β⌝ with relative clauses for α and β, thus:

Every thing x such that Fx is a thing x such that Gx.

From the particular categorical ⌜Some α is a γ⌝ we have in similar fashion the existentially quantified conjunction '$(\exists x)$ $(Fx$ and $Gx)$', thus:

Some thing x such that Fx is a thing x such that Gx.

Also we immediately get straight quantification, universal and existential, since '$(x)Fx$' and '$(\exists x)Fx$, can be explained as:

(x) (if not Fx then Fx), $\quad$ $(\exists x)$ $(Fx$ and $Fx)$.

These derivations are artificial, but their existence suffices to dull one's interest in what the actual learning process may have been.

There are two attitudes toward quantification, and toward variables, that must be carefully distinguished; for their differences are subtle but far-reaching. Viewed in one way, the variable is strictly a placeholder for the constants that can be substituted for it. Such variables do not purport to refer to objects as values. The constants that may be substituted for them need not be names at all; they may belong to any grammatical category. We saw in §25 that that category had to be fixed somehow, on pain of paradox; but it does not have to be fixed as the category of names, or of singular terms. When its variable is conceived thus *substitutionally*, a universal quantification counts as true if and only if the open sentence following the quantifier comes out true under every substitution for the variable; and an existential quantification counts as true if and only if the open sentence comes out true under some substitution.

Objectually construed, on the other hand, the variable refers to objects of some sort as its values; and these need not even be objects each of which is separately specifiable by name or description. This is how variables are understood when we give the quantifiers '(x)' and '$(\exists x)$' the classical readings 'everything x is such that' and 'something x is such that'.

Substitutional quantification differs from objectual not only in being available to other grammatical categories besides that of singular terms. It differs still in its truth conditions when applied to singular terms. A universal quantification in the objectual sense can be falsified by some individually unspecifiable value of its variable, while the same universal quantification in the substitutional sense remains true; and an existential quantification in the objectual sense can hold true by virtue of some unspecified value, while the same existential quantification in the substitutional sense fails for lack of a specifiable example. But these divergences tend to be unobtrusive, hinging as they do on unspecifiable examples.

Ruth Marcus construes quantification substitutionally, and so, less explicitly, did Leśniewski: she for reasons having to do with modal logic, he for reasons of nominalism. Some writers, careless of the distinction between use and mention of expressions, are hard to sort out. Eclectic readers have read Whitehead and Russell's quantification as substitutional on the strength of some forthright passages, but dogged reading of Whitehead and Russell supports the objectual interpretation.

The variable of the 'such that' construction, which is in effect the relative pronoun, is a substitutional variable at its inception. The words 'is a thing x such that' are learned by an equivalence transformation that is explicitly substitutional in character. And this variable, surely, is the variable at its most primitive. It is a regimentation of the relative pronoun. Variables begin as substitutional.

Once the relative clause or 'such that' construction has done its important work of siring quantification, a vital change takes place in the character of its pronoun or variable: it goes objectual. Since the categorical construction ⌜An α is a β⌝ is learned through such examples as 'An apple is a fruit', 'A rabbit is an animal', it would be inappropriate to read '(x) (if Fx then Gx)' in the substitutional way as meaning merely that every substituted name that verifies 'Fx' verifies 'Gx'. It is unnatural if not absurd to imagine names, or singular descriptions either, for all apples and rabbits.

I see this switch from substitutional 'x' to objectual 'x' as an irreducible leap in language learning. We already noticed this leap in part when we pictured relative clauses as wandering into categoricals where they could not be eliminated by the substitutional equivalence transformation. The further point to notice now about this leap is that along with forsaking eliminability it forsakes the substitutional status of the variables themselves.

Once the substitutional variable goes objectual, it goes objectual with a vengeance. It becomes the distilled essence of ontological discourse. When we talked in simple categoricals, we talked in limited ranges: all dogs are animals, all rabbits are animals, some apples are red, without prejudice to what objects there may or may not be apart from animals and apples. But the x and y of quantification are anything.

Quantification is a welcome encapsulation of the referential apparatus. Once a theory is formulated in quantificational style, its objects of reference can be said simply to be the values of its quantified variables. This of course is explicit in the intended readings of the universal and existential quantifiers: 'everything x is such that', 'something x is such that'. And the convenience of this encapsulation becomes evident when you try to say in some other way what the objects of a theory are. If you say they are the objects named by the singular terms, you omit objects that you might want to include even though individually unspecifiable: various electrons and transcendental numbers, perhaps, if not also some remote grains of sand and star dust. Also you run against the question what terms to count as singular terms and which of these to count as naming.

Taking other lines, you may say that the objects of a theory are what the general terms are true of; or, again, what the pronouns can refer to. These versions do amount pretty much to saying that the objects are the values of the quantified variables; but quantification is conveniently graphic and explicit.

Quantification, in the form in which we have come to know and love it, is less than a hundred years old. Still it is in principle a combination and excision of preexisting idiom. It can be paraphrased into old and ordinary English. By considering what steps could lead the small child or primitive man to quantification, rather than to the less tidy referential apparatus of actual English, we arrive at a psychogenetic reconstruction in skeletal outline. We approximate to the essentials of the real psychogenesis of reference while avoiding inessential complications.

Seeing the referential apparatus as epitomized in quantification, we see it as consisting essentially of two sorts of device: there are the quantitative particles 'every' and 'some', as applied to general terms in the categorical constructions, and there are the variables or pronouns as used in abstracting new general terms in the form of relative clauses. The relative clause and the categorical thus stand forth as the roots of reference. The objectual variable is an outgrowth of these two roots, not of one alone; for the variable of the relative clause begins as substitutional.

§27. *Quantifying over abstract objects*

I have been hoping to deepen our understanding of reference, and of object, by an imaginative reconstruction of how people and peoples might achieve reference to objects. I have been trying to devise a series of plausibly easy stages, plausibly short leaps, that might bring the emulous individual or the evolving society to the point of handling something tantamount to quantification and thus referring in the fullest sense to objects of some sort.

Such a study commands added interest where it touches abstract objects, since we tend to be mystified regarding their nature and doubtful regarding their credentials. The first abstract objects to gain recognition are perhaps properties, or attributes. One already has general terms, concrete general terms, to start one down the garden path. One has then only to treat such a term as a singular term; the attribute is what this singular term names. And we already noticed some general terms that slip over into the role of singular term remarkably easily: we say 'Hoboken is square' and we say 'Square is a shape'. Such terms beat a path for the others.

Anything we can say about an object is treated as assigning an attribute to it. This highly creative doctrine of attributes is the inevitable outcome of two factors. One factor is the shift from concrete general to abstract singular; it is thus that we project attributes from all our general terms. The other factor is the relative clause; for it assures a general term encapsulating anything we can say about an object. We thus end up with attributes corresponding to everything we can say about anything.

I should like now to develop my hypothetical series of stages of language learning more explicitly, to the point where these abstract objects enter the ontological scene unequivocally as values of quantified variables. In order to set aside some extraneous issues, however, I shall treat not of attributes but of classes. The only difference is that classes are taken always to be identical if they have the same members, whereas attributes are not always taken to be identical when they hold of exactly the same objects. A trouble with attributes is that we are never told, or anyway not in clear enough terms, what the further conditions of their identity might be. Talk of attributes does fit ordinary language more closely than talk of classes, and I think I know why. I suspect, as usual, a lingering tendency to confuse use and mention. One feels the attributes to be different when one feels dissimilar attitudes toward the corresponding relative clauses. Still classes do accomplish all the scientific work that the attributes would accomplish, since the one trait that sets attributes apart from classes is imprecision. And finally, what matters for present purposes, a class has all the abstractness of an attribute. By coping with classes we shall be coping with the full problem of abstract objects. So let us speculate on the possible linguistic origins of set theory.

A curiously myopic view of this matter has been manifesting itself of late.[1] There is a hindsightful reaction, after two generations, to the paradoxes of set theory. The new view is that even before the paradoxes it was not usual to suppose there was a set, or class, for every membership condition. The view is defended by citing Cantor as having already entertained certain restraints on the existence of classes before Burali-Forti published the first of the paradoxes. Fraenkel has undercut this argument by claiming that Cantor had already sensed paradox.[2] What is myopic about the view, in any event, is that it looks back only to the first systematic use in mathematics of the word 'set'

1. E.g. in D. A. Martin's review. See also my reply.

2. See a biography by Fraenkel in Cantor, p. 470.

or 'Menge', as if this were uncaused. For surely it is traditional to talk as if everything we say about an object assigned an attribute. It is evident nowadays, further, that this attitude toward attributes is involved in paradoxes just like those of set theory. And it should be evident that classes, or sets, are wanted simply as the extensional distillates of attributes. It is implausible that Cantor or anyone else would narrow this universe of classes for other than sophisticated reasons, either nominalistic scruples or fear of paradox.

In trying to imagine a psychologically feasible genesis of set theory I shall start with general terms, including the relative clauses, and use substitutional quantification. The genesis will not be a matter of eliminative definitions. It will proceed by irreducible leaps, but plausibly short ones.

The namelessness of apples and rabbits was what showed us that our variables had gone objectual. But we might continue to use substitutional variables for other purposes. In fact it is precisely in the use of substitutional variables for *general* terms that I can imagine an origin of an ontology of attributes, or classes. I shall now develop this idea.

Quantification over bodies owes its origin in part, I suggested, to the previous learning of the categorical construction ⌜Every α is a β⌝. This line was forced on me by the objectual character of the quantification. If a variable can be held to substitutional status, on the other hand, our pupil can easily learn to quantify it without ever thinking of the categorical construction. He observes that universal quantification, of the substitutional kind, commands assent if and only if each substitution instance commands assent. He observes further that the quantification commands dissent if a substitution instance does. Once he has persuaded himself of these regularities in the behavior of the speakers of the language, he has gained a pretty good command of universal substitutional quantification. There remains just one limited blind quarter that he must master later in theory-laden ways: if none of the instances of the quantification command dissent, but some command abstention, then he will not know in general whether the quantification will command dissent or abstention. The situation is like that of conjunction (§20).

Existential substitutional quantification is parallel. It commands dissent if and only if each substitution instance commands dissent, and it commands assent if some substitution instance commands assent. It has its blind quarter where none of the instances command assent but some command abstention; here the quantification may command either assent or abstention. The situation is like that of alternation.

So we see, well enough, how substitutional quantification can be learned. Different styles of substitutional quantification can be learned in this way, corresponding to different syntactical categories of instantial expressions—different categories of expressions substitutable for the quantified variables. The syntactical category that interests me here is that of general terms, for it is by substitutional quantification with respect to general terms that we can simulate set theory. In so far as we think of this substitutional quantification as simulating objectual quantification, we are thinking of the general terms as simulating abstract singular terms: simulating names of attributes, or of classes.

Summarizing then, I shall sketch our pupil's past and present progress down this garden path. He learns his first variables, we saw (§24), by learning relative clauses; for, in my caricature, the relative clause has the form 'thing x such that Fx'. These first variables are substitutional, for he learns the relative clause in predicative position as a substitution idiom. Independently of this he learns also the categorical copula, without variables, as joining general terms: $\ulcorner$Every α is a $\beta\urcorner$. Next, we saw, he combines these two idioms, on the strength of an analogy between relative clauses and general terms. The relative clause is analogous to a general term in that it is learned in predicative position; this is the very position that gave the relative clause its intelligibility as a substitution idiom in the first place. So, pursuing this analogy, our pupil slips relative clauses into the categoricals. Thenceforward the relative pronoun, or 'such that' variable, figures as an objectual variable rather than a substitutional one; for the animals and other bodies are mostly nameless. Our pupil is engaging in quantification now, for categoricals with relative clauses give quantification; and it is objectual quantification over bodies. All this happened by the end of §26.

Next he learns another sort of quantification, whose variables take the positions of general terms. Formally, structurally, it resembles the objectual quantification that he already learned. But he learns it differently. Objectual quantification came of a fusion of two idioms, the categorical copula and the substitutional 'such that'; and the fusion turned the substitutional variable objectual. On the other hand the new quantification can be learned whole, without any such fusion, because it is substitutional and is to stay substitutional until further notice. It is learned, we saw, by learning how the conditions of assent and dissent relate these quantifications to their substitution instances.

Of course this learning is facilitated by the outward resemblance of this quantification to the objectual quantification that was already learned. This resemblance has also a more profound effect: it induces a resemblance between general terms and singular terms, since general terms are the substituends for these substitutional variables and singular terms are substituends for the objectual variables. The resemblance makes the general terms feel like names of something or other, and our pupil is not going to put too fine a point on it. Such is the unconscious hypostasis of attributes, or classes. Our pupil has progressed well down the primrose or garden path.

§28. *Set theory*

In recounting this supposititious psychogenesis in terms of quantification, I am adhering to my caricature. My conjecture is that our actual learning of the ordinary idiomatic apparatus runs parallel to this caricature. But I gain visibility by bypassing the sinuosities of ordinary language.

The substituends for the substitutional variables are the general terms. Among these are the relative clauses, or 'such that' clauses. As substitutional quantification simulates objectual quantification, then, so the 'such that' clause simulates a class name. The clause 'thing x such that Fx', strictly a concrete general term, takes on the guise of the abstract singular term '$\{x: Fx\}$', 'the class of all things x such that Fx'. The 'such that' construction takes on the guise of class abstraction.

Let us promote the simulation by writing the 'such that' clauses as class abstracts, '$\{x{:}Fx\}$'. The old substitution transformation that explained the 'such that' construction now reappears as the set-theoretic law of *concretion*. As a substitution transformation it equated 'Fy' with 'y is a thing x such that Fx'. As law of concretion it equates 'Fy' with '$y \in \{x{:}\ Fx\}$'. The old copula of predication, 'is a', has become 'is a member of', or epsilon.

Classically, quantification over classes is objectual, class abstracts are singular terms, and epsilon is a two-place predicate or relative general term. I am now suggesting an avenue to this classical estate from humbler beginnings. The 'such that' construction is a humble enough accomplishment, and so is substitutional quantification governing general terms.

The set-theoretic law of *comprehension:*

(1) $(\exists Z)\,(x)\,(x \in Z \mathrel{.{\equiv}} Fx)$

is forthcoming. It assures a class for every membership condition. For we have, to begin with, the tautology '$(x)\,(Fx \equiv Fx)$'. Transforming its left side by the substitution transformation, we get:

(x) (x is a thing y such that $Fy \mathrel{.{\equiv}} Fx$),

or, in our new notation,

(2) $(x)\,(x \in \{y{:}Fy\} \mathrel{.{\equiv}} Fx)$.

But this is a substitution instance of the substitutional existential quantification (1). So (1) follows.

(1) combines substitutional and objectual quantification. The combination is not new. It has been made by Wilfrid Sellars and more recently by Charles Parsons and in my *Philosophy of Logic* (pp. 93f).

In the above proof of (1) I assumed that (1) is *closed*, or devoid of free variables. I assumed that there are no free object variables hidden along with 'x' in the clause of (1) that is represented as 'Fx'. For suppose there were a further free variable 'w'. Let us rewrite 'Fx' accordingly as 'Gwx'. The desired law (1) then runs thus:

(3) $(\exists Z)\,(x)\,(x \in Z \mathrel{.}\!\equiv Gwx)$

and its basis (2) thus:

(4) $(x)\,(x \in \{y\colon Gwy\} \mathrel{.}\!\equiv Gwx)$.

But open sentences, sentences with free variables, are not true or false; rather they are *satisfied,* or not, by values of their free variables. If a substitutional quantification is open, as (3) is, then what it calls for is not a truth condition but a satisfaction condition. The satisfaction condition for an open substitutional existential quantification, such as (3), is just this: a value of the free variable ('*w*' here) satisfies the quantification if and only if it satisfies some instance thereof, obtained by putting some class abstract for the '*Z*'. (Parsons, p. 235.) Now every value of '*w*' does indeed *satisfy* (3), because every value of '*w*' satisfies the instance (4) of (3).

What are true are thus not (3) and (4) themselves, but their universal closures:

(5) $(w)\,(\exists Z)\,(x)\,(x \in Z \mathrel{.}\!\equiv Gwx)$,
(6) $(w)\,(x)\,(x \in \{y\colon Gwy\} \mathrel{.}\!\equiv Gwx)$.

In this way the law (1) of comprehension is still forthcoming in its full generality, with and without hidden free variables. The truth condition for substitutional quantification is what yields (1) when there are no hidden variables, and the satisfaction condition for substitutional quantification is what yields (1) when there are hidden variables.

The unrestricted law of comprehension is a famous source of paradox. But there is no such worry here, because of the two styles of variables; the class variable '*Z*' cannot supplant the individual variable '*x*'. We have two types, in Russell's sense.

Let us clearly understand where our pupil now stands. He seems to be talking of classes. He even says he is, though we may question the meaning of his saying so. At any rate his law of comprehension is unrestricted, so far as classes of first type are concerned—classes of individuals. Yet all that is really afoot is substitutional quantification with concrete general terms as substituends. Can he get the benefit of all these classes without the onus of really assuming them?

He cannot.[1] There are elementary truths of set theory that fail under the substitutional interpretation. The simplest example I know is what we may call the *law of unit subclasses:* Any class that has members has some unit subclasses. This is unacceptable when substitutionally interpreted. For, thus interpreted, what it says is that whenever we can write a class abstract or relative clause that is true of a lot of individuals, we can write another that is true of exactly one of those individuals.

It is unacceptable for the same reason that substitutional quantification over physical objects was unacceptable (§26). It says that whenever we can somehow demarcate a multiplicity of physical objects we can also specify a unique sample; and this assumption is about as unwelcome as assuming a distinctive designation for every physical object. If we were prepared to make such assumptions, we could as well accept substitutional quantification across the board.

It is interesting to observe where an apparent proof of the law of unit subclasses from (5) bogs down. From (5) we make four successive steps of deduction, as follows:

(7) $(w)(\exists Z)(x)(x \in Z .\equiv. w = x)$,

(8) $(Y)(w)(w \in Y . \supset (\exists Z)(w \in Y \cdot (x)(x \in Z .\equiv. w = x)))$,

(9) $(Y)((\exists w)(w \in Y) \supset (\exists w)(\exists Z)(w \in Y \cdot (x)(x \in Z .\equiv. w = x)))$,

(10) $(Y)((\exists w)(w \in Y) \supset (\exists Z)(\exists w)(w \in Y . (x)(x \in Z .\equiv. w = x)))$.

This last line is a precise formulation of the law of unit subclasses. Where then have we gone wrong?

The fallacy occurred in the last step, where I switched '$(\exists w)(\exists Z)$' to '$(\exists Z)(\exists w)$'.[2] Commutation of consecutive existential quantifiers (and of universal ones) is eminently allowable in ordinary logic, but not when one quantifier is objectual and the other substitutional.

1. Discussion with Gilbert Harman and Oswaldo Chateaubriand started me on this track.

2. I am indebted here to William Talbott.

For, picture '*Y*' as some class abstract or relative clause that is true of various individuals but true of none that can be uniquely singled out. Each such individual *w* will satisfy:

$$w \in Y \cdot (x)\,(x \in \{y\colon w = y\} \;.\!\equiv\!.\; w = x)$$

and hence will satisfy:

$$(\exists Z)\,(w \in Y \cdot (x)\,(x \in Z \;.\!\equiv\!.\; w = x)\,).$$

Thus

$$(\exists w)\,(\exists Z)\,(w \in Y \,.\, (x)\,(x \in Z \;.\!\equiv\!.\; w = x)\,).$$

Yet not

(11) $(\exists Z)\,(\exists w)\,(w \in Y \,.\, (x)\,(x \in Z \;.\!\equiv\!.\; w = x)\,),$

since this would require there to be a closed class abstract, devoid of free variables, that singles out some such individual *w* uniquely.

Commutation of consecutive universal quantifiers fails along with that of existential ones. For, since '$(\exists w)\,(\exists Z)$' amounts to '$\sim(w)\,(Z)\sim$' and '$(\exists Z)\,(\exists w)$' amounts to '$\sim(Z)\,(w)\sim$', commutativity of the universal quantifiers would imply commutativity of the existential ones.

There is a still worse anomaly. Each member *u* of *Y* satisfies the open sentence:

$$\{y\colon u = y\} \text{ is a unit subclass of } Y \,.\, u = u.$$

Hence, by our satisfaction condition for substitutional quantification, each such *u* satisfies also the open sentence:

$$(\exists Z)\,(Z \text{ is a unit subclass of } Y \,.\, u = u).$$

Yet '$(\exists Z)$ (Z is a unit subclass of Y)' without the '$u = u$' is simply (11), and thus false. It is intolerable that such deletion of a vacuous clause '$u = u$' should reduce a satisfiable sentence to a false one.

In classical set theory, which is wholly objectual, the law of unit subclasses of course goes without saying; nor is there any trouble about switching consecutive existential quantifiers, or universal ones. But the combination of objectual quantification for individuals and substitutional quantification for classes is like oil and water. Substitutional quantification is inadequate for classes unless we are prepared to make an assumption tantamount to substitutional quantification over individuals as well. And surely for individuals, physical objects, the case for objectual quantification was conclusive. Quantification over physical objects was objectual because of its categorical root, in sentences like 'Rabbits are animals' that treat of individually nameless objects. Of course each rabbit and even each grain of sand can in principle be systematically specified and accorded a descriptive name, e.g. with help of spatiotemporal coordinates. But such an artifice is wildly irrelevant to genetic considerations, and has its place only at the level of a conscious reworking of explicit scientific theory.

I do not see this clash, or crash, as refuting my genetic speculations. I see it as conflict in the actual genetic forces. We saw another such debacle already in §25, when we found that something like Russell's paradox could be generated simply by overdoing the substitutional idiom that gives us relative clauses. It is a historical accident that that paradox was not noticed before the rise of set theory, and it is a historical accident that the present clash was not noticed more explicitly than it seems to have been.

Once it is noticed, steps need to be taken in the way of revision: revision not of the psychogenetic theory, but of the set theory or other science to which those psychogenetic processes have led. Any scientific theory has its psychogenesis, and occasionally a theory does prove to demand revision. The present case is remarkable only in lying so deep.

The revision that I would expect is a revision of status of the quantification over classes: a shift from substitutional to objectual. Already, indeed, we have seen such a shift from the originally substitutional variable of relative clauses to the objectual variable of quantification over physical objects. When we reconstrue class quantification as objectual, the hypostasis of classes is complete. Class abstracts attain the full stature of abstract singular terms.

Schematism has carried us far from the human situation. Let us restore something of the connection. Mostly people do not explicitly quantify over classes at all. Occasionally they speak of properties or attributes in ways that answer nearly enough, for our schematic purposes, to quantification over classes. Also they will say things that involve no explicit mention of classes or attributes but that come nevertheless to call for quantification over classes when we paraphrase them into economically schematic language. The Geach-Kaplan example, 'Some critics admire only one another', is a good case of this.[3] It is only the mathematicians and kindred spirits that go beyond these sporadic implicit uses and press the class apparatus on principle. It will be to such spirits, almost exclusively, that the holding or failing of the law of unit subclasses or the law of commutation of quantifiers or related laws will make any detectable difference even implicitly. Even these mathematicians, moreover, will mostly be heedless of an option between substitutional and objectual set theory, and heedless of a switch from one to the other. We, however, can tell that they have switched, however unconsciously. For we may be sure that nominalism is right psychogenetically: classes or attributes are first conceived through substitutional variables for general terms. And then, when we catch the mathematician conforming to the law of unit subclasses and the like, *we* know that he has gone objectual.

So the distinction is absurdly remote from the typical language learner. But it concerns us because we are interested in the theory of language learning for the light that it may throw on the nature of scientific theory.

§29. *Sour grapes*

Our loss, in giving up the substitutional view of class quantification, is less acute than might at first be supposed. We must recognize that even substitutional quantification, for all its reassuring air of easy access, is not altogether a free ride. It owes

3. See my *Methods of Logic*, third edition, p. 238 of later printings. It was stated incorrectly in early printings of the third edition.

its easy intelligibility to its transparent truth conditions: a universal quantification is true if and only if each substitution instance is true, and an existential quantification is true if and only if some substitution instance is true. But those truth conditions, for all their transparency, are not eliminative definitions. Adoption of substitutional quantification over classes was thus already an irreducible assumption of some sort, and who is to say that it is not an indirect assumption of some sort of new objects such as classes? There is a problem here of foreign exchange: what borrowings in terms of substitutional quantification are equivalent to what explicit borrowings of objects of objectual quantification?

By way of further consolation it should be noted that those truth conditions of substitutional quantification were not really so transparent anyway, if the class abstracts that are used as substituends happen to contain class quantifiers in turn. For, think what might happen. A substitutional quantification over classes has its truth conditions, we tend to think, in the truth conditions of those simpler sentences that are substitution instances of that quantification. But the fact is that those substitution instances need not be any simpler. The class abstract that we substitute for the quantified variable, in getting one of the substitution instances, can itself contain a quantification more formidable than the one we are instantiating.

The important distinction emerges between *predicative* and *impredicative* class abstracts. The impredicative ones contain bound class variables. (There is more to the distinction when classes of classes are at hand; but this will do for now.) As long as we adhere to predicative class abstracts, the circularity that we just now observed does not occur. Classical set theory, however, demands the impredicative line. Adopting it, we would have had to recognize that those substitutional truth conditions afford only a partial semantical account of the quantifiers. For a full truth definition we would have to revert to Tarski's style, as if the class quantifiers were objectual. This reflection may help further to reconcile us to our objectual attitude toward class quantification. But it is still not to deny that class quantification was substitutional in origin. I am persuaded that abstract objects owe their acceptance to what is essentially substitutional quantification, cast in natural language.

Substitutional quantification has already been widely regarded as inadequate for classical set theory, but for a wrong reason. People have reasoned from indenumerability, as follows. Substitutional quantification allows no nameless classes as values of the variables. Since the available expressions are denumerable, then, substitutional quantification allows only denumerably many classes. Any of the classical versions of set theory, on the other hand, assumes indenumerably many classes. The class N of the natural numbers itself has indenumerably many subclasses.

Because of our genetic approach, we have been picturing classes only of physical objects. Still, numbers must somehow make their entry in due course. For the moment let us anticipate them, so as to meet the above argument on its own terms.

Actually there is no clear contradiction between substitutional quantification and indenumerability.[1] No function f enumerates all classes of natural numbers; this Cantor shows by citing the class $\{n\text{: not } (n \epsilon f(n))\}$ as one that is missed by the enumeration f. Does substitutional quantification require the contrary—that some function f enumerate all classes of natural numbers? At first it seems so: it seems we could produce f by lexicographically numbering all class abstracts. However, the function that numbers the abstracts is not quite the required f; it is a different function, g. Its values are abstracts, whereas the f that would contradict Cantor's theorem would have classes as values. After all, the substitutional character of our quantifiers and variables does not mean that the classes *are* the abstracts; the substitutes for the variables are not names of abstracts but the abstracts themselves, the purported or simulated names of classes. The function f that would conflict with Cantor's theorem is rather the function such that $f(n)$ is the class *named* by the nth abstract $g(n)$. But there is no prospect of specifying such a function in the notation of the system; for the naming relation is notoriously unspecifiable, on pain of the familiar semantic paradox of Grelling

1. I am indebted here to a remark of Saul Kripke's.

or Richard. The apprehended contradiction over Cantor's theorem is just that same semantic paradox.

The reasoning that I have just rebutted was needlessly devious. With a little permuting and shortcutting it comes down to the observation that there is a class that is named by no abstract; namely the class

(1) $\{x$: x is an abstract and not a member of the class it names$\}$.

This way of putting the matter cuts through the talk of numbers and indenumerability and treats directly of the expressions and classes of them. The paradoxical character becomes explicit, since (1) itself is visibly an abstract. And the paradox is humdrum, hinging visibly on the naming relation.

I agree that a satisfactory substitutional foundation for classical set theory is not forthcoming. But I have been at pains just now to separate good from bad reasons.

There is also a bad argument to the opposite effect, purporting to show that substitutional quantification *is* adequate to classical set theory and indeed to any theory. This argument appeals to the Skolem-Löwenheim theorem. According to that theorem, any consistent theory has a model in the natural numbers. And obviously the natural numbers are amenable to substitutional quantification, there being a numeral for each.

To see the Skolem-Löwenheim theorem in its proper perspective, let us bypass the talk of models and turn to fundamentals. Consider a set of truths regarding an indenumerable domain. The theorem tells us that we can reinterpret those truths as a set of truths regarding a denumerable domain. Reinterpret? If we are allowed to reinterpret every sign capriciously, we can make any strings of signs say anything we like. No; the idea of the theorem is that we are to disturb only the terms and the range of the variables, while preserving the meanings of the truth-function signs and quantifiers. In short, we keep elementary logic and change the rest. But then what the Skolem-Löwenheim theorem tells us is merely that quantificational and truth-functional structures are by themselves insensitive to the distinction between denumerable and indenumerable. The theorem tells us merely that the distinction is not that elementary, and that it can be expressed only with help of one or another *term*—epsilon, for instance, or, for that matter, 'denumerable'. Quantificational and truth-functional structures are by themselves insensitive, of course, to most distinctions; they are sensitive to the distinction between finite and infinite, as it happens, and insensitive to distinctions between infinites.

When phrased in the old way in terms of models, the theorem engendered a feeling that indenumerability is somehow a matter of point of view or of perverse interpretation. This feeling tends to subside when we recognize that what is involved is only the degree of elementariness of the concept. Why should the theorem suggest that only natural numbers are needed as values of our variables?

I should like also to ask what the notion of substitutional quantification amounts to even as applied to the natural numbers. I do so a few pages hence.

§30. *Identity and number*

We imagined in §15 a primitive inception of identity as a mere temporizing locution, helping to sustain a prolonged ostension. This accounted for the identity sign only as restricted by some general term, such as 'apple', and flanked by demonstratives: 'This is the same apple as this'.

Now that we are picturing the child as learning various linguistic constructions by language-dependent similarities, we readily picture him as learning unrestricted identity along the following lines. He comes by degrees to appreciate that whoever assents to sentences ⌜$\alpha = \beta$⌝ and ⌜α is a γ⌝ will assent also to ⌜β is a γ⌝. In the end he becomes disposed to assent to ⌜$\alpha = \beta$⌝ when he can in general see his way to assenting to ⌜β is a γ⌝ on the heels of ⌜α is a γ⌝ for arbitrary γ. He is not using quantification over classes here; the regularity of behavior that he comes to appreciate and to emulate of course does not get put into words at all. He may, however, be presumed to have mastered the relative clause. This is valuable for the vast range of general terms that it affords him in the role of γ above. Thanks to relative clauses, ⌜α is a γ⌝ can in effect be any sentence containing α.

Even here, where identity stands free of any restrictive term, a relativistic account of identity retains a certain force. For the semantic standard of identity just now set forth remains relative to the words available in forming the terms γ. When some additional general terms accrue to the language, a sentence ⌜$\alpha = \beta$⌝ that counted as true by the above standard could be turned false. The fineness of individuation of our universe of discourse, or of values of our variables, varies with the richness of our supply of general terms. Individuation is in the eyes of the beholder, and varies with the strength of his lexical spectacles.[1]

When class quantification is at hand, '$x = y$' becomes definable in familiar fashion as meaning that y is a member of every class of which x is a member. This is of course not the route of learning. Still, for the while that class quantification retains its primeval substitutional character, this definition just sums up the semantic characterization of identity that went before: the characterization by exhaustion of relative clauses.

Armed with the identity predicate, let us now turn to the natural numbers. These are definable in set theory in various familiar fashions, but not within the low level of set theory that we have thus far considered: the theory of classes of individuals. Anyway, those set-theoretic definitions of number are notoriously irrelevant to psychogenesis. What perhaps does reflect the learning of number pretty well, when due allowance is made for the artificiality of the formalism, is numerical existential quantification as defined with help of identity. We have:

$$(\underset{0}{\exists} x)Fx \equiv \text{not } (\exists x)Fx$$

$$(\underset{1}{\exists} x)Fx \equiv (\exists x)\,(Fx \text{ and } (\underset{0}{\exists} y)\,(Fy \text{ and not } (y = x))\,),$$

$$(\underset{2}{\exists} x)Fx \equiv (\exists x)\,(Fx \text{ and } (\underset{1}{\exists} y)\,(Fy \text{ and not } (y = x))\,),$$

1. See my *Set Theory and Its Logic*, p. 15. For bringing the point to bear in the present connection I am indebted to Geach, "Ontological relativity and relative identity."

and so on. There is no class quantification here at all; just objectual quantification over individuals.

What now of quantification over numbers? Substitutional quantification bogged down for classes, but it seems perfectly suited to the natural numbers, since each has a numeral to designate it. As before, we do not define these quantifiers, but we know how they can be learned. '$(n)Gn$' holds if and only if 'Gn' holds under all substitutions of numerals, and '$(\exists n)Gn$' holds if and only if 'Gn' holds under some substitutions.

'Gn' here stands for any sentential context of 'n'. But what contexts are there? Thus far, 'n' can take only the subscript position beneath the existential quantifier. We can say:

$$(\exists n)\,(\,(\exists_n x)Fx \text{ and } (\exists_n x)Gx)$$

to mean e.g. that there are as many fellows as girls. But what of arithmetic, with all its sums, products, and equations? In principle a learning routine can be laid out, however absurd from a human point of view. People will assent to '$(\exists_{n+0} x)Fx$' in just the circumstances in which they will assent to '$(\exists_n x)Fx$'. This generality warrants assent to the identity '$n + 0 = n$', according to the identity standard noted a few paragraphs back; for the singular terms α and β of that paragraph can be '$n + 0$' and 'n', and the general term γ can be 'thing m such that $(\exists_m x)Fx$'.

By a similar fantasy we may picture the learning of '$m + (n + 1) = (m + n) + 1$'. This, with '$n + 0 = n$', gives the classical recursion for addition. The recursions for multiplication and exponentiation can be handled similarly, and also the equations '$2 = 1 + 1$', '$3 = 2 + 1$', etc. that define the numerals. Elementary number theory is thus well begun.

The drab reality is different, and less indicative. Children are taught prefabricated algorithms intensively in elaborate institutions. Otherwise they would not learn arithmetic. The routine of observation and emulation of adult usage that we have just now been imagining would bog down for want of example. But I think the above account shows the steps that would be required in learning arithmetic under ordinary conditions of language learning, if it could be done. It would be done if there were a more general tendency among adults to chat about sums and products within earshot of the young. Not that this is desirable.

We talk of numbers as of things, to the extent of quantifying over them. We discourse elaborately of them, but mostly in isolation from the rest of the world; they enter into operations and equations with one another. When they do relate to the world beyond arithmetic, they do so at first in just one way: in saying how many things are thus and so, $(\exists x)Fx$. Numerical expressions resist other contexts. If we ask whether 3 is a class, and whether 5 is a member of it, we draw a blank or worse. This is why the set-theoretic interpretations of number enjoy such freedom and variety: there are no preconceptions apart from special contexts. And it is just those special contexts, the algorithmic ones and '$(\exists_n x)Fx$', that are accounted for in the above caricature of number learning. I think the caricature captures essential traits of what really goes on.

This numerical setting is opportune for some further reflections on substitutional quantification, its comforts and its vexations. A comfort of it is the unproblematical character of the learning of it. The natural numbers seem peculiarly amenable to it, thanks to their numerals.

A substitutional number theory can even be combined with objectual quantification over individuals without conflict. The troubles over classes in §28 hinged on our *relative* specification—relative to a free objectual variable—of an otherwise unspecifiable class. Those troubles do not extend to natural numbers, because each of these is absolutely specifiable by a numeral.

But now consider: where is the comfort? If the natural numbers are not to stop short, infinitely many numerals must be available to substitute for the numerical variables. What are these numerals? We cannot say that each is a physical object, an inscription, for then the supply stops short. Can we say they are shapes? Shapes in what sense? Not in the sense of classes of the inscriptions that are the physical realizations of the shapes, for then we are in trouble again over short supply; unrealized shapes would reduce to the null class and thus be indistinguishable from one another. And not in the sense of analytical geometry, where a shape becomes a class of classes of pairs of real numbers, for there is no comfort in explaining numbers in terms of numerals that are explained ultimately in terms of real numbers.

The dilemma can be stated more simply and generally. A substitutional explication of arithmetical quantification brings no ontological economy to elementary number theory; for either the numbers must run short or the numerals are infinitely numerous. If the explanatory talk of infinitely many numerals is itself to be understood in turn in terms of substitutional quantification, we confront a problem at least as grave as the one about numbers; and if on the other hand our talk of infinitely many numerals is to be understood in terms of objectual quantification, we might settle uncritically for objectual quantification over numbers in the first place.

The truth conditions of substitutional quantification over numbers can indeed be made clear by talking only of numerals and their substitution, but the numerals, if they are to serve this purpose, must be as abstract as the numbers themselves. Expressions generally, if they are to be infinite in supply, might as well be identified with their Gödel numbers; no other view of them offers any visible reduction in degree of abstractness.

Between a substitutional and an objectual account of quantification over the natural numbers, then, there is a material difference only insofar as the substitutionalist is prepared to forswear the arithmetical law that every number has a successor. He would be in the position contemplated by Goodman and me in 1947. Some number would be the last, though our substitutionalist would not know which; it would depend on the facts of existence of inscriptions, past and future. His would be an arithmetic with an unknown finite bound—an arithmetic of the sort that Essenin-Volpin has called the theory of feasible numbers.

Language is learned in a succession of leaps, and the unconscious transition from substitutional to objectual quantification over numbers is one more such leap. It is completed, to all intents and purposes, when the learner finds himself believing that every natural number has a successor. This crucial step is abetted by ignorance: nobody knows how high the actual numerical inscriptions are destined ever to reach, whereas everyone knows how to top any given one. And finally, having gone unconsciously objectual over numbers, he will not boggle at objectual quantification over classes. It was somewhat thus, we may imagine, that abstract objects made the scene.

§31. *Higher types*

We have thought about classes of individuals, in some sense. Classes of physical objects, perhaps; or perhaps also, by now, of numbers. What then of classes of classes? Resuming our psychogenetic speculations, we may or may not picture our aging pupil as having caught up with the troubles over the laws of unit subclasses and commutation of quantifiers and thus been persuaded to switch to an objectual doctrine of first-type classes. In either case we may picture the classes of second type as emerging in the manner of their first-type precursors: through substitutional quantification with relative clauses as substituends. Early in life our schematic pupil learned our schematic relative clause, the 'such that' construction, by learning to equate the predication 'y is a thing x such that Fx' to 'Fy'. Now similarly he will learn relative clauses of the next type by learning to equate the predication 'Y is a class X such that FX' to 'FY'. Relative clauses are general terms, but the relative clause that he has now learned is an abstract general term: 'class X such that FX'. Next he would learn second-type substitutional quantification, using a new style of variable whose substituends are these abstract general terms. But also he would repeat his old trick of pronouncing relative clauses as class abstracts. Thus these abstract general terms become class abstracts of second type, hence doubly abstract singular terms. He would take to saying, not 'Y is a class X such that FX', but '$Y \epsilon \{X: FX\}$'. His new substitutional quantification is now nominally a quantification over second-type classes. Finally he might finish the job by reconstruing this quantification as objectual, because of the law of unit subclasses or similar troubles.

The caution that was sounded at the end of §28, by way of inducing some sense of contact with reality, is of course doubly needed now. Natural cases of implicit quantification over higher-type classes are hard to find in ordinary discourse and even in nonmathematical science. Illustrations comparable to the Geach-Kaplan example (§28) are not forthcoming for higher types. We happy few who broach that domain at all learn it from systematic treatises. My purpose in still pressing on with the construction of a fictitious learning process is to understand better why set theory came about: how it represents the fairly natural if not inevitable continuation of what is already at work at lower language levels.

The imaginary development just now described can be repeated for further types, step by step. The types can be taken either as mutually exclusive or as cumulative; it is merely a question of taking the ranges of substituend expressions exclusively or cumulatively. If they are taken cumulatively, there is no difficulty in the way even of transfinite types. Class variables of type ω admit as substituends the class abstracts of all finite types.

I have represented set theory as rooted in substitutional quantification. Further I have represented it as rooted in a theory of types, by imagining analogical extensions from type to type. But I have represented it also as outrunning its substitutional interpretation. Equally, and more promptly, it would lose any type-theoretic structure. The analogical extensions were matters surely of unconscious analogy, bringing wave after wave of new classes or attributes; and these would naturally just accrete to the growing universe without preservation of strata. Scruples over mixing the levels would be as unlikely as scruples over impredicative classes. Thus I do not see Russell's theory of types as dormant common sense awakened. Still I do see it as somewhat akin to that. I see Russell as making cleavages that were not there before, but that nevertheless bear a significant relation to the psychogenesis of classes or attributes. The relation is roughly this: the nth type comprises just the things that would be forthcoming if our unconscious receptivity to analogical extension were unnaturally restricted to n iterations. But this way of phrasing the relation is rough in two respects, one minor and one major. The minor point is that the phrasing fits rather the cumulative types than the exclusive ones, and it is the exclusive types that were historically Russell's. The major point is that this way of phrasing the relation neglects impredicative classes. The impredicative classes would seem to have no better pedigree, genetically speaking, than might be claimed for a class that violated the theory of types. So let us not cease to see the theory of types for what it is: partly a formalization of natural origins, but primarily an artifice for blocking the paradoxes.

There are of course alternative artifices—Zermelo's and the rest. These seem to be more remote from likely psychogenetic patterns, for there is no evident way of getting them started in terms of substitutional quantification. In the case of Zermelo's system,[1] or that of von Neumann and Bernays,[2] or my "New foundations,"[3] what makes substitutional quantification hard to apply is that in those systems there is no deciding in general whether a class abstract succeeds in naming a class or not; whereas in the theory of types every class abstract that is grammatical at all is taken as naming a class. In the system of my *Mathematical Logic*,[4] and again in the system that has been variously referred to as von Neumann-Quine and Bernays-Quine and Kelly-Morse,[5] the obstacle is different. In these systems every abstract does name a class, but there is no evident way of accommodating the distinction between sets and ultimate classes.

If our notion of the realm of classes or attributes was developed first along lines somewhat congenial to the theory of types, as we have been imagining, then further steps to the other set theories are easily pictured. First, within the theory of types, there is the unconscious shift in the interpretation of quantification over classes: a shift to the objectual. Once the theory of types is seen objectually, the other set theories become intelligible as deliberately fashioned alternatives.

Zermelo's system and others are sometimes rendered as *pure* set theory: set theory without individuals. In that setting there is no evident impediment to substitutional quantification, except that the truth condition is impoverished as always by im-

1. See my *Set Theory and Its Logic*, §38.
2. Ibid., §43.
3. Ibid., §40.
4. Ibid., §42.
5. Ibid., §44.

predicative classes. However, set theory plays its part in our overall theory of the world only by going impure.

§32. *Psychogenesis summed up*

We have reviewed the genesis and development of reference. Our review may be taken as applying to either the individual or the race, since it is imaginary in any event. An early phase of reference, perhaps the earliest worthy of the name, was the universal categorical, as in 'A dog is an animal'. Thus far no variable and so no substitution. The next phase was the relative clause, or 'such that' construction. Here was the inception of the variable, and a substitutional variable this emphatically was; for the relative clause was learned by means of a substitution transformation. But the contexts that could be resolved by this transformation were of course just the contexts where the relative clause was least needed, since eliminability implies dispensability. The relative clause turned ineliminable and indeed indispensable when it slipped into the position of one of the general terms in the universal categorical. Here, moreover, its variable turned objectual. Objectual quantification was thus at hand and objective reference was in full sway. There was reference to physical objects as values of quantified variables.

Quantifiers and variables are alien to the vernacular, and so, for that matter, is 'such that'. Yet I find the foregoing account plausible in its essentials, especially as a factual account of learning by the child. Surely his learning of the relative clause begins with his getting the knack, however unconsciously, of a substitution transformation, since this transformation is the one evident link between a relative clause and the freestanding sentence that is its prototype. 'I bought Fido from a man who found him' and 'that I bought from a man who found him' go into each other by substituting 'that' for 'Fido' and vice versa. My use of the 'such that' form for the relative clause merely simplifies matters and brings the substitution relation into sharper relief by obviating the idiomatic readjustment of word order in the relative clause. The child might have learned the 'such that' construction more quickly than the classical relative clause, if it had been in the air.

Perhaps he learned interrogatives earlier than relative clauses: 'who?' and 'what?' earlier than the relative pronoun 'that'. This is just a question of the detail of his mastery of the substitution transformation for relative pronouns, since the same substitution transformation underlies the interrogative pronoun.

The variable, like 'such that', is a departure from the vernacular on my part to simplify the rules. Nested clauses generate ambiguities of cross-reference otherwise, we saw, that are resoluble only by opportunistic paraphrases if at all. Variables might well, like 'such that', have been easier for the child to learn than the vernacular style of relative clauses and pronouns. In invoking them I schematize my conjectures about language learning, but what I am conjecturing is that the child learns the vernacular in the same way, in between mastering the inessential complications that are bypassed in the schematism.

When I impute a shift from substitutional variables to objectual, I am speculating at two removes; for the child does not really know about variables, let alone any distinction between substitutional and objectual. Still I am schematizing what I think is the real development. The child learns the relative pronoun through the substitution transformation; it is in this sense that I say his variables are substitutional at first. But when he gets to saying sentences of the form 'Everything that we salvaged is in the shed', 'Everything I find is mine', he is not counting on individual designators; substitution is no longer the point. It is in this implicit way that he may be said to have switched from substitutional to objectual variables, though really no variables are in sight. In seeing this as a switch I am assuming that the universal conditional 'Everything that . . . is . . . ' was learned by slipping relative clauses into the categorical; but this seems reasonable.

The quantifier is another departure on my part from the vernacular. With its variable it conveniently encapsulates several vernacular locutions, such as 'Everything that . . . is . . . ', 'There are . . . ', 'Something is . . . '. Quantification is translatable into these idioms and vice versa, with the aid of truth functions. When I speak conveniently of the child as learning quantification, therefore, the lie is distinctly a white one.

Talk of classes is another such heuristic departure on my part. The vernacular usually has 'attribute' or 'property'. In cleaving to classes I avoid the dark side of attributes, while continuing to examine the learning of abstract terms and the hypostasis of abstract objects. I think the resulting account is true to that learning process, excluding the dark side, the side that concerns the individuation of attributes; and this exclusion is after all pretty vacuous, since the individuation of attributes remains forever pretty much unlearned.

So my account of the learning of first-type set theory is meant as a schematized account of the child's actual learning of the ordinary language of abstract terms. This learning is eased, I think, by two blurs: the blur between the concrete general and the abstract singular use of a word, and the blur between substitutional and objectual variables. Variables, I urged, are at first substitutional—which is to say, more literally, that the relative pronoun is learned by a substitution transformation. The child may learn them as easily when general terms are the substituends as when singular terms are the substituends. The blur between general and singular terms is partly a help here, no doubt, and partly a consequence. Thus far, then, we have brought the child abreast of the relative pronoun of abstract reference; that is, in effect, the variable of 'such that' with abstract values. It is abstract reference or abstract values only by courtesy, still, for the variable is only substitutional. The next step in the unconscious simulation of abstract reference is quantification of this variable, or the vernacular equivalent—partly hidden, perhaps, in such contexts as the Geach-Kaplan example. This could be learned by easy analogy with the previously acquired quantification over individuals (or the vernacular equivalent). To the child of course it is no conscious analogy, but just more of the same. Here we have a blur between the substitutional variable and the objectual, since the quantification over bodies had one of its roots in the universal categorical and was thus implicitly objectual. The new abstract quantification has no such root in the categorical, and may thus stay substitutional for a time. As a reward for this, moreover, it admits of an easily learned truth condition in lieu of a root in the categorical. This substitutional truth condition brings firmness to the idiom, analogically learned at first, of quantification over virtual classes (or the vernacular equivalent).

In a subtle way this substitutional quantification, with general terms as substituends, depends on the prior objectual quantification over individuals also quite apart from the matter of analogy. For it needs the relative clauses, or 'such that' clauses, as its substituends; and 'such that' is a variable-binding operator whose variable has already been lured over into objectual status by the demands of categorical contexts.

Numbers are learned in counting and perhaps other contexts, and then the child learns substitutional quantification over them (in effect) on the analogy of what has gone before. The substitutional truth condition does its good work again here.

Already there have been short ontological leaps into the abstract. These class quantifiers and number quantifiers, for all their disarmingly substitutional character, are not eliminably defined. Still there need be no thought, at first, of anything so monstrous as abstract objects—numbers, classes. And observe now with what cunning these monsters insinuate themselves. The numerical quantifier may as well be seen as objectual, I suggested, if we allow each number a successor. The class quantifier went objectual when we admitted commutation of quantifiers and therewith the law of unit subclasses.

Again no awareness of a distinction between substitutional and objectual quantification is to be imputed to the child, nor to the layman. With some laymen the question of accepting the successor law never arises. To them, then, this distinction between two kinds of numerical quantification does not apply. Other laymen may commit themselves in response to questioning. If they do, their acceptance of the successor law may be expected.

In the case of classes our criterion of objectual quantification was acceptance of the law of unit subclasses and the commutation of successive existential quantifiers and of successive universal ones. To test a lay subject by these criteria would require clever questioning. Failing that, we must put our subject down as one to whom the distinction between substitutional and objectual quantification over classes does not even implicitly apply.

The problem of extorting an implicit commitment to impredicative classes is much the same. We can expect the subject to use relative clauses that are the vernacular equivalent of impredicative abstracts, or to admit of being led by interrogation into using them. But it is hard to construct nontechnical occasions for his using such clauses as substituends for variables.

When we press on to higher types, we have little to do with language-learning processes in child or laymen. I already stressed this point in §31.

§33. *Past and future*

The preceding section summarizes the child's acquisition of the apparatus of reference as I imagine it. Reference is my main concern in this book, but we might glance at other aspects of cognitive discourse. What of sentences about past and future?

If we are to deal with the child's passage to sentences about the past, we must consider what to do about memory. To remember someone's name is, typically, to be disposed to say it when queried in his presence. Memory in this sense is substantially a matter of observation sentences again, and no past tense. 'Red' and 'Mama' and 'Addison Sims of Seattle' are all learned alike. Forgetting someone's name is forgetting a bit of language.

Thus what we ordinarily speak of as memory is already covered in some small part at the level of ordinary observation sentences where no past tense is involved. What now of the past tense? Alongside the observation sentence 'Red' or 'I see red' we may picture the report of past observation: the simple, undated 'I have seen red'. However, there is little point in speculating on how the child might acquire this particular use of the past tense, because it is so useless; it goes without saying. If the child is competent to use the word 'red', it stands to reason that he has seen red; and otherwise he is in no position to say so, however falsely. An observational report in the simple past is idle insofar as there is a presumption that its observation term was acquired by direct conditioning. Russell declared singular existence statements to be meaningless when their subjects were genuine proper names; and the reason here is the same.

So let us turn rather to reports of past observation where the term is one that may be expected to have been acquired by definition rather than by direct conditioning. Or, since we can supplant any defined term by its definiens, what the case comes to is the report of past observation where the term is complex; say 'I have seen a black rabbit'. Now mastery of the sentence consists, as always, in learning the circumstances of assent. What, then, are the cues that the child might learn for assenting to the query 'Seen a black rabbit?'? He has learned the terms 'black' and 'rabbit' by direct exposure, and he has learned attributive composition, so he will recognize any occasion for assenting to the query 'Black rabbit?' if the occasion arises. In the idiom of images we might say that those words conjure up the right image, even failing the real thing. And now I fear we may have to assume yet a little more in the way of built-in faculties; namely, a discrimination on the child's part between two kinds of images, images of fancy and images of memory. This sounds like Hume, who appealed lamely to vivacity as the distinguishing trait. Memory is muted sensation and fancy is muted memory. But we should like to dementalize the formulation. An image is a neural event inducing a state of readiness for an appropriate impingement pattern. Such a pattern may not come, but the child is aware anyway, we now assume, of that monitory neural event itself; that is, he must be able to respond distinctively to it, and distinctively even to two varieties of it. One variety rests solely on the assembling of learned elements, 'black' and 'rabbit'. The other variety has been reinforced by enactment in some actual impingement pattern. The one rests solely on description while the other has been reinforced by acquaintance, to speak in Russell's terms. Now it is when the words 'black rabbit' induce this latter, more vigorous sense of readiness that the child may rightly assent to the query 'Seen a black rabbit?'. He is said to remember seeing one.

There are two conditions for learning when to assent to a sentence: the cues must be perceptible in themselves, and they must get assigned to the sentence. These present speculations about memory images have to do with the first factor: the child's cues for 'Seen a black rabbit'. The other question, how the child could learn from his elders to connect such sentences with such cues, is more easily answered. The parent rewards the child for assenting to queries regarding past observations that the parent saw the child make. Also he penalizes dissent in such cases. Also the child finds the parent reporting past observations that the child saw the parent make.

Dated reports of past observations, next, can be smoothly accounted for if we imagine for convenience of schematism that a calendar clock is in view. 'Black rabbit on February 9 at 10:15' is a plain observation sentence that commands assent under any impingement pattern that happens to include among its features a glimpse of a black rabbit and a suitable glimpse of the hands of the calendar clock. If we throw in the past-tense verb, 'I saw', we have a sentence of the same type as the preceding example 'I have seen a black rabbit'; it differs only in that its observation term is more complex, applying no longer simply to animals but to animals and clocks in combination. Adding one more equally minor complication, we can accommodate observation reports that are both dated and located. We have merely to imagine that a signpost is visible saying where we are.

At last we have arrived at protocol sentences, as they were called in the Vienna Circle. They are the repository of scientific data. Thanks to their dates, they are eternal sentences, like those of scientific theory generally—or they become so when we drop the personal idiosyncrasy of the 'I saw' and report simply 'Black rabbit on February 9 at 10:15 in Sever Quadrangle'. The dropping of the 'I saw' is a primitive step of inference from a report of observation to an eternal sentence integral to the theory. These eternalized reports comprise the archives of scientific evidence, or would do so in a bookkeeper's dream world.

What of the future tense? As the past tense hinged on memory, so the future must hinge on expectation. Expectation, at its most primitive, is supposed to hinge on induction from past experience. If episode *a* was followed by episode *b*, then after an episode *a′* similar to *a* the subject expects one *b′* similar to *b*. Now this much is already provided by our earlier theory of images. According to it, an episode leaves a trace from which a partially similar episode can raise an image. Just let the one episode be the temporally inclusive one, *a* followed by *b*. Then a subsequent episode *a′* similar to *a* is partially similar also to the tandem pattern *a* followed by *b*, and so raises a tandem image *a′* followed by *b*'. It is perhaps this, primitively, that constitutes the expectation of *b*' on the strength of *a*'.

This account is suited nicely to the blind expectation that future successions will resemble past successions. It gives only what we already saw (end of §7) in the enhancement of salience by the sound of a word. The word 'dog' was sounded in view of a dog, and afterward it serves to induce the dog image and enhance the salience of any further dog. Does this mean that it makes us *expect* a dog? I think it does, primitively; and perhaps our first use of the future tense has no more than this as its tentative cue. But our elders penalize us for poor predictions and reward us for good ones, and so our use of the future tense is eventually brought under control. The details of this mechanism remain rather baffling, and not without interest; for prediction, after all, is the payoff of scientific theory itself.

The steps of language learning that I have conjectured lead up to that portion of language that is used in natural history—in the kind of science that is sometimes called empirical as *opposed* to theoretical. Measurement might be worked in; for we have considered the acquisition of the natural numbers, and set theory shows the way from them to the real numbers. But what of theoretical posits, hypothetical forces, hypothetical particles?

I hold open some hope for that forbidding domain by thinking of the kinetic theory of gases as a paradigm case. Boyle's law, to begin with, makes sense at the level of natural history; for it can be explained as relating expansible tanks and thermometers. The subsequent positing of molecules, then, can be seen as essentially just one more extrapolation along the time-honored lines of similarity. But it is a matter, to begin with, not of similarity of the molecules to anything; it is the expansible tank that is similar to a confined swarm, say, of bees. Afterward, by further analogy, the molecules are posited as analogues of the component bees.

Even a perfected psychology of science would not aspire to keep causal track of the minds at the advancing front of natural science. This would be no great loss; for the psychological theory is concerned rather with the basic phenomenon of scientific knowledge than with its latest variations. And anyway the minds at the advancing front are themselves aware of what they are doing.

§34. *Ontological sophistication*

As summarized in §32, the child's acquisition of the apparatus of reference stopped short of any deliberate ontologizing on his part. But the boundary is not sharp. The learner progresses by analogy and even by crude simplicity considerations, largely unawares. The scientist or philosopher who in a scientific spirit undertakes to clarify, organize, or simplify his ontology is doing more of the same, but doing it better and in full awareness.

So it is with the set theorist, venturing ever upward and outward on his lofty ontological limb. The farther he ventures, the less it matters even to natural science, let alone common sense. But besides that steep limb there are other ontological branches to consider.

One striking scientific improvement on common sense is the notion of a scattered four-dimensional physical object with temporal as well as spatial parts. Naively considered, Mama smiling and Jumbo on the rampage are nothing of themselves; there are just Mama and Jumbo, who smile or romp from time to time. So body-minded are we, we do not think of the Evening Star and the Morning Star as phases or aspects of Venus; they simply are Venus, and Venus may be referred to by the one term or the other depending on the time of day. Similarly for Carnap's example of Rumber, or Titisee;[1] the lake was one and the same, but was appropriately referred to by the one term or the other depending on the weather. Similarly for Dr. Jekyll and Mr. Hyde; they would probably be reckoned not as complementary temporal parts of a whole and nameless man, but as an identical man with two names appropriate to two of his modes or moods. Bodies, in a first unsophisticated ontology, have no parts but bodies. The more general and more sophisticated notion of physical object enables us to talk more systematically of the variously changing bodies, by giving the stages of the bodies an ontological status on a par with the bodies themselves. We can identify a fit of ague with the concurrent temporal segment of the victim's body. We can identify a battle, for that matter, with the physical object that is the sum of the appropriate temporal segments of all the com-

1. *Foundations of Logic and Mathematics.*

batants. Also, as remarked, we can assimilate mass terms to singular terms, each a name of a diffuse physical object.

Less easily, colors can be accommodated too. Scarlet can be identified with the scattered totality of those surfaces whose fine structure is of such kind, or of any of perhaps several kinds, as to radiate light in the appropriate spectral band or to reflect such light selectively when illuminated in a complete mixture of frequencies. And how thick are we to take this "surface," as a physical object? Just thick enough to include this optically operative fine structure. To attack this account as a bad definition of 'scarlet' would be off the point; it is an account rather of how to fit that color into the expanded ontology.

Shapes are more stubborn than colors. Each shape, indeed, such as square, or circle, is an abstract object. However, putting these aside for the present, what about the particular squares and circles? Even these are more stubborn than colors. Can we identify a particular square with a physical object that is a sum of four suitable edges? It is not clear how thick to take the edges: there is no causal condition to resort to as there was in the case of colored surfaces. Shall we identify the square rather with the whole enclosed patch of surface? Four objections crowd in. First, the question how thick to take the surface, as a physical object, is in the same difficulty as the previous question of edges. Second, there is bound to be some irregularity at the edges, some deviation from ideal squareness, when we get down to elementary particles; and thus there is indeterminacy as to which peripheral particles to include. Third, the resort to the enclosed patch would be of no avail when we turn from squares to semicircles or other open figures. Fourth, there remains the problem of identifying a square as the same square through time.

Moreover this approach, even if successful, would accommodate only this and that particular square and not the shape square itself, on a par with the color scarlet. We accommodate scarlet as a scattered mass, and so we may, since unions of scarlet regions are scarlet. But a trouble with squares is that their unions are not in general square; nor can we even tell what squares a given union of squares is meant to be a union of, since we have by now passed the stage of counting as square only such manifolds as are visibly marked out.

One classical solution is a double ontology: matter and space. Spatial manifolds are aggregates of points as physical objects are aggregates of elementary particles; and squares are spatial manifolds. Physical objects are in space. A particular cross section of some physical object will almost exactly occupy a particular square, and indeed it will almost exactly occupy each of infinitely many almost coincident squares. There is no longer a problem of diachronic identification; a square, a particular aggregate of points, retains its identity through all time. Or, when we integrate time with space as a fourth dimension, we take squares as the appropriate manifolds in four-space. Points give way then to point-instants. Purely spatial squares, i.e. squares normal to the time axis, are on this approach instantaneous rather than diachronically identified. The everlasting square of the preceding account is still with us, but it is represented now as a three-dimensional square parallelepiped of infinite length oriented parallel to the time axis in space-time, or to somebody's time axis.

If the previous objections are now overcome, two new ones take their place. One of them has to do with the inelegance of a tandem ontology: matter and space. The other, more serious, has to do with the gratuitousness of a doctrine of absolute position. Without absolute position, spatial or spatiotemporal, an ontology of purely spatial or spatiotemporal manifolds seems incoherent.

These two objections drive us back to a renewed effort to construe the manifolds in attachment somehow to physical objects. This attachment may be contrived by means of numbers and measurement; and such is the familiar enlightened approach to the matter. A point is identified with a triple of real numbers, or, for spatiotemporal purposes, a quadruple. Squares and other manifolds are identified with the appropriate classes of such triples or quadruples, according to analytical geometry. Thus far there is no talk of physical space nor of physical objects. Finally the connection with physical objects is made by applying pure number through physical measurement. When we say e.g. that four villages are so related to one another as to form the vertices of a square, we are talking of the arithmetical relation of the distance measurements of these villages. We are saying that the pairs of measurements from any arbitrary rectangular coordinates, one pair for each village, will meet the arithmetical conditions of the vertices of a square according to analytical geometry. Ultimately we are merely saying something about the relation of the distances of the four villages from one another; namely, that four of these six distances are equal to one another and the other two are equal to each other. The excursion through coordinate systems is just a device for handling such relations systematically.

We have got rid of the ontology of manifolds, but only to find ourselves dealing with a good deal more than physical objects. Here are the numbers and their pairs and triples and quadruples and the classes of such. We have got rid of the ontology of manifolds only to take on an ontology of abstract objects. What with these and the physical objects, we have a tandem ontology as before.

It must be said in extenuation that we would have found ourselves needing this ontology of abstract objects anyway for many purposes. We would have broached it even while retaining the ontology of manifolds, as soon as we began talking of shapes: of square, circle, etc. For the manifolds were just individual squares and circles and the like; the shapes would be classes of them, and thus objects of a higher abstractness.

§35. *Ontological economy*

We have been seeing ontology as expansionist. Set theory in its higher reaches adds exorbitantly to the population of the universe, and it does so purely on ontological principle: by extrapolating single-mindedly and inexorably *ad infinitum* some guidelines that are hinted at their hither ends by the more modest and faltering ontology of common sense and natural science. Even at the level of physical objects, moreover, ontological self-consciousness has tended rather to add entities than to weed them out, if we may judge from our present survey. Surely our sophisticated universe of physical objects is denser than the naive universe of bodies. Entities are being multiplied.

Occam's stricture on such multiplication, however, is but part of a broader counsel of economy or simplicity. The generalizing of bodies to physical objects brought an important gain in simplicity of organization, by regimenting our mass terms and Heraclitus's talk of time and the river under a clean-cut pattern of general and singular terms and objective reference. Again the acceptance of numbers and low-type classes had, among other simplificatory effects, that of clarifying our talk of spatial manifolds and organizing its connections with our talk of bodies. And even the excesses of higher set theory come of a drive for simplicity, after all: a distaste for discontinuities of principle. But in the case of higher set theory one yearns for other useful and simple principles without all that fecundity.

Ontology is not always expansionist. It has its contractionist side, though we have not had occasion in these pages to observe it. By becoming clear on the nature and requirements of reference we find that some seeming entities are better bypassed by paraphrase, in the interest of not only ontological economy but simplicity of theory generally. An example is impure number, or units of measure. Ordinarily we talk of these as of objects, by names and general terms; but they are better analyzed in an idiom that relates pure numbers directly to physical objects in various ways. Again there is the whole realm of intensions, attributes, propositional meanings, unactualized possibles. As we become clearer and more explicit in ontological matters we come to appreciate the urgency of individuation principles, which are weak or wanting in the case of intensions. Also we become aware of some subtleties having to do with referential opacity, which I shall not pause over here. The result can be that we find the intensional entities to be less help than hindrance, less simplificatory than complicatory, and out they go.

The vernacular use of the referential apparatus is indeed careless and prodigal of objects, if we read it in a literal-minded ontological way. 'There is one thing about him that I don't like'; 'He and Elizabeth have so many interests in common'. How many things are there about him altogether, liked and disliked? How many interests has he altogether, how many has Elizabeth, and how many are in common? We use those idioms without countenancing such questions, and the questions may be blamed as justly on an emergent literal-mindedness of ontology as on an abortively ontological vernacular. But when ontology steps forward to take these matters systematically in hand, the effect is apt to be rather contractionist than otherwise.

Talk of ontological economy or extravagance makes sense only within a prescribed framework of allowable grammatical constructions. It would be meaningless to dismiss vast categories of objects by invoking novel linguistic forms and constructions and declaring these to be innocent of referential intent. It would be meaningless for want of a standard of referential intent. We give content to the ontological issue when we regiment the language of science strictly within the framework of the logic of truth functions and objectual quantification. In so doing we limit the resources of other than ontological kind, and are thus enabled fairly to assess and compare any costs or savings in ontology from theory to theory. I remarked early in §29, for instance, that substitutional quantification, far from being ontologically innocent, is simply ontologically inscrutable except through some stated translation into this objectual idiom.

Such regimentation accounts for the ontological expansion lately noticed. Some of the burden came to be reckoned to ontology that had previously been accommodated in incommensurate ways through miscellaneous constructions.

Mostly in this book I have speculated on causes, not justifications. I have asked how our ontological notions are possible, not why they are right. Even in the case of bodies, those prototypical objects of reference, I offered no hope of justification. I entertained no thought of translating talk of bodies into talk of sense impressions, as Russell and Carnap dreamed of doing a half century ago. I asked how, given our stimulations, we might have developed our corporeal style of talk. And I asked how we developed our abstract, set-theoretic style of talk. One could ask, in the same spirit, how we developed our religious talk, and our talk of witchcraft, and our talk of analyticity and logical modalities. If we managed to reconstruct these causal chains of language learning, we would find that every here and there the learner had made a little leap on the strength of analogy or conjecture or confusion; but then the same seemed to be true of our learning to talk of bodies. In short, I speculated on causes and not on values. Sheep are caused and goats are caused, and they are caused in similar ways.

In the past two sections I have been concerned no longer with the subject's learning of the referential apparatus, but with his deliberate ontologizing. But even here I have been concerned more with the nature and meaning of what he is doing than with what he or we ought to do. How then should we settle our ontology?

§36. *Relative empiricism*

That last question is little less than the general question of scientific method: the question how best to develop an inclusive scientific theory. We want to maximize prediction; that is, we want a theory that will anticipate as many observations as possible, getting none of them wrong. We develop the theory by progressive observation and correction. When we have to modify the theory to accommodate a wayward observation sentence, we have various possible corrections from which to choose; and here the guiding considerations are simplicity and conservatism. We prefer the correction that makes for a simpler theory, by our subjective standards of simplicity, unless the other alternative is more conservative, that is, a less drastic departure from the old theory. But a big simplification can warrant a fairly drastic departure. We arbitrate between these two interests, simplicity and conservation. They are related *dialectically,* to borrow a term from my students.

In some measure, conservatism is imposed by our poverty of imagination rather than freely chosen. But it can also be a deliberate matter of prudence, a matter of adhering to the tried and true where we can instead of betting on wild hypotheses. As we go on modifying theory to accommodate observation, the consideration of simplicity of theory may indeed so far outweigh conservatism that we give up our old belief in witchcraft; perhaps also religion; perhaps modal logic; but there are limits.

These two forces, the force for simplification and the force for conservatism, are already at work in a primitive way in our learning of language, if my causal speculations have been near right. I have pictured the process as a series of short leaps, each made on the strength of similarities or analogies. In this pursuit of similarities or analogies we see the force for simplification, and in the shortness of the steps we see the force for conservation. Learning language, learning gradually to quantify over bodies and eventually over abstract objects, is one phase of a continuing process that goes on to embrace also the learning and even the further developing of high scientific theory. We are working up our science from infancy onward. Each of the leaps of language learning that I have pictured is a private little scientific revolution, another step in the development of a system of the world. If the leap is one that conduces to simplicity in the child's evolving conceptual scheme, then normatively speaking it is good scientific method on his part, however unconscious. If it is a short leap, then again it is good, on the score of conservatism.

I have called short leaps conservative. It is more illuminating to call them empiricistic. They are governed by this maxim of *relative empiricism:* Don't venture farther from sensory evidence than you need to. We abandoned radical empiricism when we abandoned the old hope of translating corporeal talk into sensory talk; but the relative variety still recommends itself. We recognize that between the globally learned observation sentences and the recognizably articulate talk of bodies there are irreducible leaps, but we can still be glad to minimize them, and to minimize such further leaps as may be required for further reaches of ontology. The maxim has evident practical value, in minimizing our liability to backtracking when need arises for a change of theory.

The maxim would have us try to preserve the substitutional interpretation of quantification over abstract objects, if I have been right in supposing that this was genetically the prior interpretation. Considerations of overall simplicity of theory could outweigh this consideration and sustain the objectual interpretation, but at any rate there should be a deliberate weighing of considerations.

The substitutional interpretation of quantification over abstract objects appeals to the nominalist temper. This appeal is a manifestation of relative empiricism, for the urge to nominalism is itself just that. But the wishful nominalist must beware, we saw, of overestimating the ontological innocence of substitutional variables. In general the values of the objectual variables of a theory may fairly be said to exhaust the ontology only if the theory is couched in terms solely of predicates, truth functions, and objectual quantification. If there are irreducible additional devices—modal operators, say, or substitutional quantification—then there is no assessing its ontology except relative to some stated translation.

Very well, the nominalist may reply, let us grant that substitutional quantification does not make a clean ontological sweep; still something is gained. Substitutional quantification over numbers, for instance, gets explained in terms of expressions and substitution rather than in terms of abstract objects and reference. But here again we must disappoint him; for we reflected in §30 that the expressions needed as substituends are entities as abstract as the numbers.

Our thwarted nominalist may still cleave to substitutional quantification where he can, as a way of tempering ontological excesses. Nominalism aside, he might hope by substitutional quantification to reduce the extravagant ontology of real numbers or of set theory to that of elementary number theory by framing truth conditions for substitutional quantification in terms of Gödel numbers. But a reductive program of this sort should be seen as a project less of nominalism than of Pythagoreanism. It is a matter not of prizing the concrete and abhorring the abstract, but of tolerating natural numbers and abhorring most of the transcendentals. It is as if to say, with Kronecker, "God made the natural numbers; the rest are human handiwork."

However, this more modest objective is obstructed too. Substitutional quantification over classes was found in §28 to conflict with objectual quantification over physical objects—or to conflict, anyway, with whatever good reasons there might be for adhering to objectual quantification over physical objects.

This threat to the substitutional interpretation of class quantification could be met if we could see our way to interpreting our quantification over physical objects substitutionally too. Our reason against this was the namelessness of most rabbits, all grains of sand, all electrons. But are these really nameless? Every physical object is specifiable with help of spatiotemporal coordinates, and so can be named by a singular description. This desperate resort was too farfetched to be interesting as long as we were speculating on the psychological origins, but does it bear consideration now that we are ontologizing on our own?

I think not, still. Consider the motivation. We want to interpret our quantification over physical objects substitutionally in order to remove the obstacle to substitutional quantification over classes. And why do we want substitutional quantification over classes? The motive was quasi-nominalistic, and ultimately a matter of relative empiricism. But if relative empiricism speaks for substitutional quantification over classes, it speaks also for objectual quantification over physical objects—these being the versions that are closest to the respective genetic origins, if my genetic speculations have been right. And anyway the device of numerical coordinates seems a poor way of buttressing substitutional quantification over physical objects, when we recall the quandaries of substitutional quantification over numbers.

Charles Parsons has proposed for quantification over classes a *semisubstitutional* compromise between the substitutional and the objectual account. For the truth of an existential quantification in this sense it is no longer required that there be a true substitution instance; there need only be a substitution instance that contains free objectual variables and is satisfied by some values of them. Correspondingly a universal quantification, even if devoid of free variables, no longer claims merely the truth of all substitution instances devoid of free variables; it requires further that all substitution instances containing free objectual variables be satisfied by all values of them. This version of class quantification restores the law of unit subclasses and the usual permutability of quantifiers, and it resolves the related anomaly of the vacuous clause (§28). Its truth condition lacks the charm of the transparent truth condition of strictly substitutional quantification, and of course it suffers equally in the presence of impredicative abstracts. Still it does retain something of the desired nominalistic aura that is wholly lacking in the objectual version, and I see no reason to doubt that it meets the needs of set theory.

references

T. G. R. Bower, "The object in the world of the infant," Scientific American 225, no. 4 (Oct., 1971), pp. 30-38.

Georg Cantor, *Gesammelte Abhandlungen mathematischen und philosophischen Inhalts,* E. Zermelo, ed., Berlin, 1932.

Rudolf Carnap, *Der logische Aufbau der Welt,* Berlin, 1928. Translation, *The Logical Structure of the World,* University of California Press, 1967.

———, "Testability and meaning," Philosophy of Science 3 (1936), pp. 419-471; 4 (1937), pp. 1-40.

———, *Foundations of Logic and Mathematics,* University of Chicago Press, 1939.

Noam Chomsky, "Quine's empirical assumptions," in Davidson and Hintikka, pp. 53-68.

Alonzo Church, *Mathematical Logic,* mimeographed, Princeton University Mathematics Department, 1936.

Charles Darwin, *The Origin of Species,* 1859; facsimile, Harvard University Press, 1964.

Donald Davidson, "Truth and meaning," Synthese 17 (1967), pp. 304-323.

——— and Jaakko Hintikka, eds., *Words and Objections: Essays on the Work of W. V. Quine,* Dordrecht: Reidel, 1969.

A. S. Esenine-Volpine, "Le programme ultra-intuitionniste des fondements des mathématiques," *Infinitistic Methods* (Proceedings of Warsaw symposium, 1959), Oxford: Pergamon, 1961, pp. 201-223.

Peter T. Geach, *Reference and Generality,* Ithaca: Cornell, 1962, 1968.

———, "Quine's syntactical insights," in Davidson and Hintikka, pp. 146-157.

———, "Ontological relativity and relative identity," in Milton Munitz, ed., *Ontology,* New York University Press, forthcoming.

Nelson Goodman, *Fact, Fiction and Forecast,* 2nd ed., Indianapolis: Bobbs-Merrill, 1965.

——— and W. V. Quine, "Steps toward a constructive nominalism," Journal of Symbolic Logic 12 (1947), pp. 105-122.

Morris Halle, "Phonology in generative grammar," Word 18 (1962), pp. 54-72.

Richard J. Herrnstein, "Superstition," in W. K. Honig, ed., *Operant Behavior,* New York: Century-Crofts, 1966.

Edwin B. Holt, *Animal Drive and the Learning Process,* New York: Holt, 1931.

E. H. Lenneberg and J. M. Roberts, "The language of experience," International Journal of American Linguistics, supplement, 1956.

Ruth B. Marcus, "Modalities and intensional languages," Synthese 13 (1961), pp. 303-322.

D. A. Martin, review of Quine's *Set Theory and Its Logic,* Journal of Philosophy 67 (1970), pp. 111-114.

Charles Parsons, "A plea for substitutional quantification," Journal of Philosophy 68 (1971), pp. 231-237.

I. P. Pavlov, *Conditioned Reflexes,* Oxford University Press, 1927.

C. S. Peirce, *Collected Papers,* Cambridge: Harvard, 1931-1958.

Jean Piaget and Bärbel Inhelder, *La Genèse des Structures Logiques Elémentaires,* Geneva: Delachaux, 1959.

W. V. Quine, *Methods of Logic,* 3rd ed., New York: Holt, 1972.

——, *Word and Object,* Cambridge: M. I. T., 1960.

——, *Set Theory and Its Logic,* Cambridge: Harvard, 1963, 1969.

——, *Philosophy of Logic,* Englewood: Prentice-Hall, 1970.

——, "Reply to D. A. Martin," Journal of Philosophy 67 (1970), pp. 247f.

Gilbert Ryle, *The Concept of Mind,* London: Hutchinson, 1949.

Wilfrid Sellars, "Abstract entities," Review of Metaphysics 16 (1963), pp. 627-671.

——, "Classes as abstract entities and the Russell paradox," ibid. 17 (1964), pp. 67-90.

Nathan Stemmer, "Some aspects of language acquisition," in Y. Bar-Hillel, ed., *Pragmatics of Natural Languages,* Dordrecht: Reidel, 1971.

Leonard Troland, *Fundamentals of Human Motivation*, New York: Van Nostrand, 1928.

Ludwig Wittgenstein, *Philosophical Investigations*, Oxford: Blackwell, 1953.

J. Z. Young, *An Introduction to the Study of Man*, Oxford: Clarendon, 1971.

Paul Ziff, "A response to 'stimulus meaning'," Philosophical Review 79 (1970), pp. 63-74.

index